# Medieval Teachers of Freedom

Medieval debates over "divine creation" are systematically obscured in our age by the conflict between "Intelligent Design" Creationists and Evolutionists. The present investigation cuts through the web of contemporary conflicts to examine problems seated at the heart of medieval talk about creation. From three representative authors we learn that the doctrine of divine creation is supposed to invite understanding of the relation between artistic freedom and natural necessity, of the very essence of causality, and thereby of the nexus between experience (our world of empirical determinations) and reality (the absolute indetermination of eternal being). Most importantly, medieval scholarship shows us that the problems it addresses are originally inherent in the understanding itself, whereby the question of being emerges as inseparable from the question of interpretation.

**Marco Antonio Andreacchio** was awarded a doctorate from the University of Illinois for his interpretation of Sino-Japanese philosophical classics in dialogue with Western counterparts and a doctorate from Cambridge University for his work on Dante's Platonic interpretation of religious authority. Andreacchio has taught at various higher education institutions and published systematically on problems of a political-philosophical nature.

# Anglo-Italian Renaissance Studies
Edited by
Michele Marrapodi

**Shakespeare, Politics, and Italy**
Intertextuality on the Jacobean Stage
*Michael J. Redmond*

**Italian Culture in the Drama of Shakespeare and His Contemporaries**
Rewriting, Remaking, Refashioning
*Edited by Michele Marrapodi*

**Theatre, Magic and Philosophy**
William Shakespeare, John Dee, and the Italian Legacy
*Gabriela Dragnea Horvath*

**Shakespeare's Poetics**
Aristotle and Anglo-Italian Renaissance Genres
*Sarah Dewar-Watson*

**Shakespeare, Caravaggio, and the Indistinct Regard**
*Rocco Coronato*

**Shakespeare's Ruins and Myth of Rome**
*Maria Del Sapio Garbero*

**Medieval Teachers of Freedom**
Boethius, Peter Lombard and Aquinas on Creation from Nothing
*Marco Antonio Andreacchio*

**The Allegory of Love in the Early Renaissance**
Francesco Colonna's *Hypnerotomachia Poliphili* and its European Context
*James Calum O'Neill*

For more information about this series, please visit: https://www.routledge.com/Anglo-Italian-Renaissance-Studies/book-series/AIRS

# Medieval Teachers of Freedom
Boethius, Peter Lombard and Aquinas on Creation from Nothing

Marco Antonio Andreacchio

NEW YORK AND LONDON

First published 2023
by Routledge
605 Third Avenue, New York, NY 10158

and by Routledge
4 Park Square, Milton Park, Abingdon, Oxon, OX14 4RN

*Routledge is an imprint of the Taylor & Francis Group, an informa business*

© 2023 Marco Antonio Andreacchio

The right of Marco Antonio Andreacchio to be identified as author of this work has been asserted in accordance with sections 77 and 78 of the Copyright, Designs and Patents Act 1988.

All rights reserved. No part of this book may be reprinted or reproduced or utilised in any form or by any electronic, mechanical, or other means, now known or hereafter invented, including photocopying and recording, or in any information storage or retrieval system, without permission in writing from the publishers.

*Trademark notice*: Product or corporate names may be trademarks or registered trademarks, and are used only for identification and explanation without intent to infringe.

*Library of Congress Cataloging-in-Publication Data*
Names: Andreacchio, Marco Antonio, 1974– author.
Title: Medieval teachers of freedom : Boethius, Peter Lombard and Aquinas on creation from nothing / Marco Antonio Andreacchio.
Description: New York, NY : Routledge, 2023. | Series: Anglo-Italian Renaissance studies | Includes bibliographical references and index.
Identifiers: LCCN 2023003346 (print) | LCCN 2023003347 (ebook) | ISBN 9781032522364 (hbk) | ISBN 9781032522371 (pbk) | ISBN 9781003405689(ebk)
Subjects: LCSH: Creation—Religious aspects—Christianity—History of doctrines—Middle Ages, 600–1500. | Creation (Literary, artistic, etc.)—Religious aspects—Christianity—History of doctrines—Middle Ages, 600–1500. | Freedom and art—History—To 1500. | Liberty—Religious aspects—Christianity—History of doctrines—Middle Ages, 600–1500. | Platonists—Europe—History—To 1500. | Philosophy, Medieval. | Boethius, –524. | Peter Lombard, Bishop of Paris, approximately 1100–1160. | Thomas, Aquinas, Saint, 1225?–1274.
Classification: LCC BT695 .A56 2023 (print) | LCC BT695 (ebook) | DDC 231.7/65—dc23/eng/20230419
LC record available at https://lccn.loc.gov/2023003346
LC ebook record available at https://lccn.loc.gov/2023003347

ISBN: 978-1-032-52236-4 (hbk)
ISBN: 978-1-032-52237-1 (pbk)
ISBN: 978-1-003-40568-9 (ebk)

DOI: 10.4324/9781003405689

Typeset in Times New Roman
by Apex CoVantage, LLC

ubi primum occurrit aliquid quod non sit nobis
commune et pecori, hoc ad rationem pertinet


(St. Thomas Aquinas, after St. Augustine)[1]


A Hilail, jamais trop tard ; et à Rose et Léon,
jamais trop tôt.

# Contents

*Prefatory Remarks: The "Poetic Telos" of the Present Study*    ix
*Acknowledgements*    xv

Introduction    1

1   "Poetic Reason" as Key to Reading Medieval Authors    15

2   Theology or Philosophy? A False Dilemma    21

3   A Universe from Nothing beyond Theology?    23

4   Medieval Scholarship as Guide in Interpretation?    28

5   Aristotle or Plato? Another False Dilemma    30

6   Introduction to the Problem of Context    33

7   Medieval Platonism beyond Intellectual History    34

8   Medieval Platonism    41

9   Medieval Platonic Hermeneutics    44

10   The Problem of Creation    47

11   Creation from Nothing?    51

12   Divine Creation as Key to Freedom    56

| | | |
|---|---|---:|
| 13 | What is Freedom? | 58 |
| 14 | Emanationism vs. Voluntarism | 62 |
| 15 | Creation and the Problem of Omnipotence | 65 |
| 16 | Logos as Key to Creation | 67 |
| 17 | The Essence of Human Freedom: Creation "from Nothing" as Divine Intellective Emanation | 71 |
| 18 | Eternity and Dialogue | 74 |
| 19 | Medieval Teachers of Freedom | 77 |
| 20 | The Philosophical Heart of Medieval Scholarship | 79 |
| 21 | The Problem of Voluntarism | 82 |
| 22 | From Intelligent Design Back to Platonism | 86 |
| 23 | Being and Nothingness | 92 |
| 24 | Evil | 95 |
| 25 | Creation and Platonic Ideas | 97 |
| | *Bibliography* | *99* |
| | *Index* | *106* |

# Prefatory Remarks: The "Poetic Telos" of the Present Study

Under the heading of "divine creation," the present study investigates the medieval-Latin "art of writing" a rediscovery of which stands as *conditio sine qua non* for any genuine understanding of the cardinal questions explored by medieval Christian scholarship. The medieval art of writing emerges as poetic counterpart of a divine correlative: divine creation.

If there is a master key to Christian medieval discourse, that key does not coincide with any of the discourse's parts, as with any conceptual apparatus, but with the *mode* of the discourse: its *spirit*. The master key is not to be sought in a modern or "scientific" manner, as our "intellectual historians" or "historians of thought" have so far done systematically, but in a classical or *poetic* manner, which is to say, in a non-reductionistic manner. The question is not if any discrete notion holds primacy among others, but *how* all notions are teleologically gathered back into pure intelligibility; and that "how" must coincide with the *art* of the writer, his art of writing, as a *poet*, a guide of discourse open to the eternal, as of philology open to philosophical verities.[2]

Our intellectual historians have tended to paint thought as "safe," grounding it in mechanisms (neurobiological, psycho-pathological, social, historical, etc.) stripped of any miraculous or mysterious grounding, as opposed to outright absurdity;[3] *de facto*, they have systematically traded the eternal ideas, natural ends and desire heralded by classical antiquity for Kantian-like ideals, values and wishes. The biblical God that early modern anti-theological ideologues of freedom had condemned as too dangerous and that later modern "existentialist" prophets of anti-Christian atheism could afford reproaching for having inauthentically shielded people from danger, can be recycled, today, as an innocuous object of décor for a society of universal commodification, where safety comes to be identified with the supreme good.

What other outcome could there be to the replacement of divine intelligence with divined unreason, than the retreat into a system of mechanically grounded and imposed rules and regulations, or a regime wherein we can all publicly pretend that our life is meaningful, while privately assuming that all meaning is couched in its "evolutionary" absence?

Abraham's dangerous God appears to have been replaced with a danger utterly devoid of divine intelligence, a danger that tends to be *accepted* as a necessary unnamable evil "beyond good and evil"; and this, in the name of a new safety provided by technology and its purported underpinning evolutionary mechanisms; a safety or salvation (*salus*) that comes to be upheld as enemy of *all* danger, which consequently comes to be shunned, both privately and publicly, until our daily life remains alienated from the two greatest dangers of all: thought and love.

The upshot of the modern rejection of the medieval art of relating to the divine perfection of our being *in dialogue*, emerges as the modern, postmodern or rather "trans-modern"[4] establishment of a new life essentially thoughtless and loveless, where thought is replaced by an opinion-making machine and love by marketable compulsion. Hence the contemporary "crisis of freedom": despairing of any natural end (*telos*) of freedom, we tend to place our freedom in the hands of custodians of safety all-too-reminiscent of Dostoyevsky's Grand Inquisitor.

It is in response to the contemporary crisis of freedom and of all ideologies appealing to it that the present study dares engage in dialogue with medieval writers as "teachers of freedom" insofar as they showed to care about freedom to the point that they did not shy away from investigating its source in the divine or unlimited perfection of being itself.

A morally and conceptually dangerous conversation with medieval teachers, such as the one proposed here, cannot but appear strange to the contemporary reader, who is best advised not to seek in the present work a system of facts and information helping us frame medieval thought within a grid of expectations peculiar to our age. The challenge faced here involves the unsettling of our certainties in the light of both an unexpected truth hiding in danger and an unusual way of relating to it. So unusual that it carries us far beyond the most daring intuitions of intellectual histories—from Alasdair MacIntyre's 1981 *After Virtue*[5] to Thomas Nagel's 2012 *Mind and Cosmos*—to a land where we are naturally free to ask questions habitually forgotten beneath the answers and their machinery of production that we usually and for the most part unconsciously take for granted.[6]

Now, our conversation unfolds through a constellation of signposts that work together in helping us rise to a place of questioning pre-dating any modern compartmentalizing of both thought and life. In that place obscured by what Walter Benjamin would denounce, if only fatalistically, as our "age of mechanical reproduction," questions are "first answers" and art is the disclosure of nature itself.

A map of signposts to be encountered along the way:

Introduction:

1. Note on Ideas and God.
2. The Problem of Accounting for the Irreducibility of Experience.

*Prefatory Remarks: The "Poetic Telos" of the Present Study* xi

3. Beyond the Dichotomy of Art and Nature.
4. The Problem of Interpreting Medieval Sources:

where, in defense of our common life experience, we begin unearthing a pre-modern interaction between art and nature, or philology and philosophy;

"Poetic Reason" as Key to Reading Medieval Authors:

where we begin unearthing a pre-modern *poetic* interaction between reason and faith;

Theology or Philosophy? A False Dilemma:

where we turn back to the classical theological dimension of philosophy;

A Universe from Nothing beyond Theology?

where the contemporary "scientific" return to the classical notion of production from nothing is exposed as epistemically and morally bankrupt;

Medieval Scholarship as Guide in Interpretation?

where our medieval sources are introduced as guides capable of freeing us from peculiarly modern blinders;

Aristotle or Plato? Another false dilemma:

where a "new" way of reading Aristotle and Plato points beyond their notorious clash;

Introduction to the problem of Context:

where "context" is (re)introduced as the foremost content of interpretation;

Medieval Platonism Beyond Intellectual History:

where the constitutional borders of intellectual history are exposed and crossed;

Medieval Platonism:

where the "Platonic soul" of medieval scholarship resurfaces as key to our reading;

Medieval Platonic Hermeneutics:

> where Boethius, Peter Lombard and Thomas Aquinas are introduced as pivotal sources to our acquiring familiarity with the Platonic soul of medieval Christianity;

The Problem of Creation:

> where Boethius guides us to investigate the question of divine creation;

Creation from Nothing?

> where Thomas Aquinas guides us to think about creativity;

Divine Creation as Key to Freedom:

> where we encounter Peter Lombard as guide to discerning freedom as problem integral to divine creativity;

What is Freedom?

> where Peter Lombard further guides us to investigate the nature of freedom;

Emanationism vs. Voluntarism:

> where medieval Platonism responds to irrationalist approaches to God;

Creation and the Problem of Omnipotence:

> where divine "omnipotence" is shown to be compatible with human freedom;

Logos as Key to Creation:

> where the medieval "Book of Causes" joins our conversation on the primal mode of production of all things;

The Essence of Human Freedom: Creation "from Nothing" as Divine Intellective Emanation:

> where freedom is found to be a divinely disclosed human problem;

Eternity and Dialogue:

*Prefatory Remarks: The "Poetic Telos" of the Present Study* xiii

where we explore the intersection of the metaphysical and ethical dimensions of Logos;

Medieval Teachers of Freedom:

where a summary is provided of foregoing findings concerning the nature of human freedom;

The Philosophical Heart of Medieval Scholarship:

where our earlier findings help us vindicate the philosophical impulse of medieval "theology";

The Problem of Voluntarism:

where the ills of voluntarism are further explored and exposed;

From Intelligent Design Back to Platonism:

where the modern appeal to "intelligent design" is exposed as false alternative to modern anti-Platonism;

Being and Nothingness:

where the problem of "nothingness" emerges as pivotal in our thinking of being;

Evil:

where the problem of evil is exposed in the light of medieval Platonism's reasoning about being;

Creation and Platonic Ideas:

where a Platonic reading of biblical Creationism challenges all modern attempts to divest medieval discourse of illuminating mystery.

At the end of our dialogical journey, we should be in the position of turning back upon the beginning to discern and appreciate it as sign that the problem of being is neither 1. rendered "objectively" absurd in opposition to "subjective" thought, as modernity has taught us, nor 2. "solved" by "being thought" by a mind apart from our own, but 3. *thinking* (or intellection) itself as the inherence of the divine in the human.[7]

The challenge of thought itself is integral to our turn to the medieval doctrine of "creation from nothing" (*creatio ex nihilo*), a doctrine that, as we shall see, calls us to recognize the universe as fundamentally intelligible, rather than renounce any living participation in perfect intelligibility under the assumption that reality is utterly indifferent to our daily plights, whether because it is, has been and always will be what it is, or because it is ineluctably changing—*beyond us*. In appealing to "creation from nothing" we will be countering all misanthropic and misological tendencies to bar the common man from living access to the *arcana* or deepest mysteries of our universe.[8]

## Notes

1 "The first occurrence of that which we don't have in common with cattle depends upon reason," with the understanding that fundamentally "reason and intellect are the same" (*idem est ratio et intellectus*)—*De Veritate* ("Of Truth"), Q. 15, Art. 1, sc. 8. All translations appearing in the present study are by its author.
2 More on this, later.
3 On the modern progressively-evident replacement of mystery with the absurd, see Sommavilla 1981.
4 I have recently coined the expression "trans-modern" to designate the contemporary, authoritarian return of value-constructive progressivism in the aftermath of the postmodern destruction of the Reason of History. See my "Trans-Modernism: Genesis of a Horror Scene," at www.youtube.com/watch?v=j0uW9uGPNfY&t=70s.
5 In the opening pages of his *After Virtue* (MacIntyre 1981), MacIntyre invites the hypothesis that we all speak, today, a language the original meaning of which has long been obscured.
6 The classical primacy of questions over answers coincides with that of thought (*contemplatio* as *theorein*) over experience. The modern tendency to conflate truth and experience, or to seek truth empirically, or as an empirical *datum*, stands as obstacle to any genuine understanding and appreciation of classical—both ancient and medieval—writers who sought truth as the creative and intelligible ground of all experience.
7 For a Neo-Thomist defense of the second alternative, see Pieper 1957, esp. 51. Notwithstanding James V. Schall's *apologia* of Pieper's reading of Aquinas, the appeal to "silence" beyond/after human speech, remains fully compatible with the irrationalism of post-modernity. A strong or radical response to that irrationalism would require a turn to discover speech as "hidden" in divine intellection even as it is manifest through human reason. See Schall 1997. Doolan 2008 (82 and 252) follows Pieper unqualifiedly and unequivocally. Doolan's "exemplar causes" (as Aquinas's *causae exemplares*) corresponds indicatively to Aristotle's "paradigms" or παραδείγματα (cf. *Metaphysics*, 1.9.991a20–31), otherwise translated as "patterns" (Doolan 2008: 46).
8 Echoing p. 33 of Burrell 1994, and in the light of his own reading of Maimonides, Gluck 1998 (esp. 253–54) argued reasonably that the exercise of our human faculties—*viz.*, free will, practical reasoning and naming/conceptualizing all things—presupposes an authoritative notion of human nature, a notion that we must regard as sacred, or believe to be divinely revealed. We need a firm sense of grounding in order to move "forward" without yielding to utter/suicidal moral relativism. Gluck reads Maimonides as upholding the doctrine of creation *ex nihilo* on merely expediential grounds, or lest people lose sight of a vision of properly human destiny. While the doctrine may very well confirm a biblical or biblical-like vision of man beyond tribal differences, if not outright warfare, the question of a higher (non-consequentialist) justification remains open.

# Acknowledgments

To the innumerable providential blessings in disguise that, while tempting us to desist from pursuing truth, challenge us to divine it at the heart of our very pursuit; to both laude and offense, but principally to the latter, both when fair and unfair, for such is the natural counter-poison to that common delusion by which what is divine forgets itself in the human.

Kyrie eleison

*Image:* Oil on canvas, by the author

# Introduction

## 1. Note on Ideas and God

In the 1930's Whitehead invited "adventures of ideas" as of useful concepts.[1] This book is an adventure, but it is also a pilgrimage *into* ideas, an exploration that rises into ideas as original seats of discourse, without taking for granted the modern, anti-Platonist notion that ideas "evolve," and that a "fixed" idea, as any correlative light in the firmament, can serve as no more than a heuristic starting point for thought—as "God's essence" does in Spinoza's *Ethics*.

At first glance, the medieval doctrine of "creation from nothing" (*creatio ex nihilo*) appears incompatible with the notion that Platonic ideas (the "absolute reality" of things) are eternal. The doctrine at hand does suggest that the world created by God does not presuppose anything but God. Yet, in stating that ideas precede the ordinary contents of our experience we are not necessarily contradicting the notion that the empirical universe presupposes nothing outside of or aside from God. To claim otherwise is to assume that ideas are not eternally in God; or that the "content" of God precludes ideas; or, to put it another way, that God is not fundamentally intelligent. But what if ideas were what God is ultimately all about? What if ideas were not extrinsic properties of God, as ideas are often said to be with respect to men?

## 2. The Problem of Accounting for the Irreducibility of Experience

Modern physics is a discipline accounting for the manner in which our empirical world "holds together," asking how the distinct properties of the discrete components or "particles" of our world are related. Yet, in the course of their experimentations and calculations our physicists found it progressively difficult to distinguish between properties and particles. Is there a "gravitational-center" or "nucleus" that underlies the properties, thereby somehow holding them together? Or is there no center providing for properties' "entanglement?" Are the properties a function of things or do they exist independently of things? Do the properties interact thanks to a "material" support, or do they interact on their own, even as we may deduce "binding laws" from their interaction?[2]

On a simply materialist reading, there must be some "objective thing" (as Descartes's *res extensa*) independent of pure consciousness that holds the properties considered by consciousness together. Call those properties "ideas" (the idea of heat, of height, of weight, of speed, of color, but also of beauty, of justice, of goodness, etc.). Now, on the reading in question, ideas would be that which we can be conscious of and which serves as middle-term between our consciousness and "things themselves." Yet, what if we admitted that ideas or properties have no real support "glueing" them together? In this case, science would pertain merely to "universally abstract" entities underlying an ordinarily illusory experience of reality. Science would be about *properties/ideas* independent of any *things*.

Whether we understand nature in terms of properties such as "waves," or things such as "particles," however, the question remains open as to the manner of constitution of our common *experience*. Whether we conclude that ideas belong to things or whether we conclude that they are merely attributed to things *a posteriori*, or from without—with the understanding that ideas/properties are what things are ultimately about—we are still faced with the need to account for ideas in the light of our ordinary *unresolved* life experience.[3] In concrete terms, properties simply cannot account for themselves; no more than any supposed material support could. To borrow academic designations, whether we are natural realists, or anti-realists/nominalists, the ultimate *justification* for our science rests upon its capacity to illuminate (not instrumentalize) our common experience rather than discover any supposed physical or metaphysical building block of experience.

Whether we posit ideas/properties aside from an underlying material world, or whether we approach them as reality itself, we still face the fundamental question of what holds the properties together, which is to say of how we are to understand properties and so how we are to *practically* relate to them. Whether ideas hold themselves together independently—eternally and spontaneously—or whether they require an "external" support to interact, how can they possibly help us walk through life? Accepting one answer or another is one thing; facing and asking life's *questions* is another. What are we to expect from answers? What more than a provocation to ask questions?

Platonically speaking, the distinction between property and thing is simply illusory: ideas are what things ultimately are, namely forms of intelligibility, rather than nominal obstacles preventing us from seeing things as they really are. The question is how experience can be guided by ideas that might otherwise be seen as utterly indifferent to the practical challenges we face everyday.

Aristotle's proposal would be to provide a radical expression to Plato's teaching of ideas in terms of "mind" (νοῦς/*nous*) that "minds itself"; or, to speak in Christian theological terms, of divine intelligence returning to itself through itself. Being would then be none other than the perfection of consciousness, or consciousness of ideas as things themselves, or of ideas as eternal constituents of being/reality; so that in that consciousness, we would all live to various degrees.

This "conclusion" is at once Platonic, Aristotelian and Christian, at least insofar as Christianity is represented by philosophers relying on Aristotle's elegant formatting of a Platonic way of life. Indeed, Aristotle's "metaphysical formulas" serve as most elegant middle term to harmonize Plato's life of contemplation and the life of Plato's (and Socrates's) pre-philosophical detractors, namely of those who live as if there were no significant ontological hiatus between sensory appearance and reality; or, to return to the terminology of medieval biblical theology (Philo's included), no "fall" from Adam's natural reason to the natural reason of uneducated men. In its latter state, natural reason begs for what classical antiquity praises as Reason of State (well beyond Aristotle's elegant formulas), lest natural reason be upheld as the sheer passion of those brutish men who are continuously driven to roll in what Cicero would call "the feces of Romulus" (*faex Romuli*).[4] Indeed, at some point, only law could prevent philosophical discourse from being instrumentalized by non-philosophers (even as law alone could not answer our most pressing questions).

Our natural reason, our "bodily" reason, must be at once *civil*, lest it mistake itself for divine reason *simpliciter*.[5] And yet, the challenge of returning to an Adamic condition is not met by merely holding body and law, as nature and art, together authoritatively. The perfect coincidence of nature and art cannot be attained mechanically, as the founders of modernity would otherwise suggest in their invocations of a "scientific method" as key to the establishment of what Machiavelli would invite as "new ways and orders" (*modi ed ordini nuovi*) and of what Shakespeare would warn against in terms of a "brave new world," namely a world in which novelty is praised over the eternal and in which bravery implicates the uprooting of virtue from nature (where nature is no longer conceived as providing standards for moderate, civil life).[6]

Canonical medieval theology is adamant about the impossibility of resolving the tension between nature and art by anything falling short of their original divine perfection, a perfection that men are not to create or re-create nominalistically (or even legalistically), but *return to*, contemplatively and thus beyond the reaches of our *vita activa*, our own doings. Our "works alone," as St. Paul would remind us, will not save us from our "corruption." To paraphrase St. Augustine, three, not two are our reasons: the natural and the civil, to be sure, but also the *revealed* or purely divine. Hence the distinction that the *doctor gratiae* borrows from the pagan Varro in Book 6 of the *City of God*, between *theologia naturalis*, *theologia fabulosa* and *theologia civilis*: natural, mythical/poetic and civil discourse, that, in all three cases, is ultimately about the divine.[7]

Varro's "three types of theology" (*tria genera theologia*) or his *theologia tripertita*, serve the Christian Bishop as stepping stones to justify the sacred theology of Christianity, a *revealed* discourse stemming directly from divine intellection to reconcile the natural and the civil dimensions of life in a way that pagan poets had failed to do.⁸ With Christianity, the mythical or poetic is thus seemingly replaced by the purely or truly divine understood as the perfection of the pagan, or the revelation of that which pagans could merely "dream" of in mythical forms. On the other hand, Augustine's Christianity somehow supersedes both pagan poetry and pagan laws, insofar as the latter are now to be interpreted in the light of a higher law. What is at stake is the administration of nature, which begs for more than *mere* poetry and *mere* laws. Nature begs for an "original" or primordial support: not one approaching nature from without, but one emerging out of the ontological ground of nature to redeem nature from its "fallen" condition.

Augustine's argument is unequivocal: pagan poetry and law failed to save us from our natural or physical compulsions. Pagan poets and statesmen failed to reconnect our bodily life to the divine life of the mind. Most dreadful, however, would be the attempt to justify the corrupt Religion of State of Imperial Rome through poetic artifices.⁹ Christianity confirms this much for us, namely that there is no merely poetic justification for corrupt laws: civil authority cannot be redeemed from its state of corruption by rhetorical acrobatics, no matter how ingenious poets become. A poetry rooted in the sacred or secret depths of nature would be needed, rather than one presupposing nature, not to speak of nature's corruption. This is precisely the "poetry" that Augustine's Christianity stands for, a sacred poetry that rises above the pagan conflict between poetry and law, to restore their original harmony and thereby to show that far from being a mere imposition upon nature, the language of authority is a "living word" generated directly out of nature's own creative ground. More personally stated, only Jesus Christ provides salvation from the mutual alienation of law and nature characteristic of decadent Imperial Rome.

Rome's corruption ultimately signifies the destruction of civil order, or a "second fall" into obscurantism, the "dark ages" decried in the fourteenth century by Petrarch—after Dante and as inspiration for generations of European Platonic humanists—in defense of a poetic life emerging out of the soul of medieval Christianity.¹⁰ In those "dark ages," nature tends to be conceived "heretically" as something devoid of mind, while mind tends to be conceived as alien to, though imposable upon nature.

While the great or not-so-great "spiritualist" heretical currents of the Middle Ages upheld the alienation of mind from nature, it is only through the lengthy and tormenting systematic repression of heresies, or as heretics began administrating the repression of heresy (i.e. where the repression took up a character betraying Gnostic-like intransigence), that the project of imposing mind upon nature came of age, first in the ideological blueprints of a modern world and derivatively in the emergence of new mercantile cities compatible with a Machiavellian and then Spinozist notion that political life and order is grounded in mercantile principles.

Now, the modern development of the heretical alienation of mind from nature into an imposition of mind upon nature, entails a modification of mind and so too the rise of a novel anti-Christian understanding of mind as being not merely unconcerned with matters of the flesh, but as serving as means to a radical reformation of the physical. Indeed, mind is to convert into a *method* to master nature, or into what would be called *ideology*.[11]

It is not enough for the founders of modernity, from Machiavelli to Kant, to revive ancient Epicurean science; Epicureanism must be converted into a public or "moral imperative" purportedly overcoming the ancient conflict between Epicureanism and Stoicism. Shakespeare himself had seen well what was at stake in this Machiavellian shift towards a new Epicureanism and a new Stoicism and thus towards a novel synthesis of the two ancient antagonists. The natural reason of Epicurus could be harmonized with the civil reason of Stoics by a new method that would *use* nature to establish a universal civil order, or a universal Regime immune to the limitations of older, authoritative regimes. For the new regime would be one of freedom, a regime grounded in freedom as irrefutable *a priori*. The price to be paid for irrefutability would be, of course, unverifiability, or the prohibition (such does it become with the likes of Immanuel Kant) of all rational access to the ground of freedom. The formal indifference that Machiavelli would manifest to metaphysical questions will necessarily manifest itself, throughout the unfolding of the "brave new world" inaugurated by the Florentine, as the outright abolition of metaphysical questions and their replacement with metaphysical hypotheses grounded in the ever-changing, elusive forces of a mechanistically-conceived nature, which is to say, a nature conceived as devoid of proper, originative intelligence.

## 3. Beyond the Dichotomy of Art and Nature

Generation or nature (φύσις/*physis*) entails pregnancy (nature is always pregnant with its fruits), gestation (nature is always at work), the emergence of something hidden, perhaps something moving, even grounding nature itself (nature appears to be always "driven"); an "active principle," as Aristotelians might put it, begging to be born.

In the respect that nature tends towards the emergence of its ground within nature's own bosom, nature is both mother and daughter of art; both generator and creature, where art is at once divinely hidden in nature (as Logos in John 1) and humanly manifest out of nature (destined to die, if only in the context of a resurrection).

With modernity, art is not originally within nature as divine art, but *becomes* quasi-divine, or pretends to be divine—it functions "as if" it were— trying to project itself within nature, mechanically. Herein the crux of the

Frankenstein project:[12] man pretending to be God, or man becoming a pretense of divinity. The new art is a "science" determining or constructing itself within a nature that is no longer recognized as either mother or daughter, but as mistress. For modern man, nature is only metaphorically a mother, while art only metaphorically depends upon nature. In reality, we regard nature as a step-mother utterly indifferent to us who only feign care for nature, as if in pretending to care we could better exploit nature.

Upon, however, turning to a medieval Christian dynamics, we could enter within the articulation art-nature, rather than admiring it from without. Thereupon we would appreciate that nature is a divine or perfect art that we return to by inventing a division between art and nature, or by abstracting ourselves in terms of art out of a nature viewed as mere generation. Why would we abstract ourselves out of nature? To see ourselves, to be sure; to find ourselves, as God's self-determination. There would ultimately be no mere generation, but immediacy in art and only secondarily mediation given which generation would be "fallen" while art would seek to emerge out of the dark pit of fallen nature. Man would then seek God, only to discover that man is God seeking himself in the context of divine creation. Of course, man could err and in an extreme case could go utterly mad, falling into the temptation of using nature as means to attain to a divine status. In this case, man would stray beyond the foolish façade of the Babel project effectively mocked in the Bible. Biblically speaking, modern man pierces that façade with an impious science, or impiety converted into a science (much as alchemy converts into chemistry) to rise to a universal madness entailed by the conceited conviction that generation is originally devoid of art and that art can be "as if" autonomous of any genesis by creating itself "as if" *ex nihilo*. In that Kantian-like "as if" lies the crux of the modern tale of madness: man can only pretend to be free in the modern sense of the term, so he must learn to conceive pretense itself as truth and truth as a self-grounding lie, as Nietzsche had shamelessly conceded.

As Hobbes's unabashedly modern account of laughter shows, modern man defines himself in conceit:[13] Hobbes's laughter signals self-complacence, rather than shame in the face of death; shamelessness, rather than modesty. Such a *modern* laughter is either simply unredeemable or it must pretend to redeem itself. It must remain crushed by death, or rebel to death in an act of mad protestation. Such are the extremes that Shakespeare's Hamlet would announce in the "nunnery scene" of a play meant to guide us to a third alternative inseparable from the play itself. To discern that alternative we would need to let go of any and all Machiavellian prejudice or expectation and perhaps even of "every hope" (*ogne speranza*, warns the door of eternal law in Dante's *Inferno* 3.9) lest any fear come to distract us from our original mandate as human beings: theologically speaking, the return of the Father to himself, through the Son; otherwise put, Resurrection through the Cross, or Ascent to the Heavens through descent into Hades. Such are the terms of a divinely poetic circle.[14]

## 4. The Problem of Interpreting Medieval Sources

*"In another way we are said to judge something through something, as through the faculty (*virtute*) of judgment; and this way we judge of truth thanks to the (uncreated) active intellect."*[15]

In our age of "critical theory" and "ideology," the classical distinction between philology and philosophy, as the one between art and nature, tends to be obscured by the rise of "historical" syntheses.[16] Philology, or what used to be thus called, stands to art—thus, to the products of human choice—as philosophy stands to the *nature(s)* presupposed by art.[17] The philologist as such orders the world of art, while the philosopher as such is bent upon making sense of the natural or necessary ground of artistic production broadly understood to include all that depends upon human arbitration. In principle, or considered holistically, philologists and philosophers should work together, lest art and human arbitration be represented as devoid of the three staple characteristics of classical, Platonic learning: system, hierarchy and teleology. As Nino Langiulli reminded us, Protagoras, Plato's philosophical adversary, conceived of learning as both systematic and hierarchical, but not as genuinely teleological, in the respect that for the Sophist's learning does not entail any journey to a desired perfection, or the Good.[18] Likewise, today's scholarship appears to have lost a sense of *telos* independent of the demands and expectations of "the times."[19] In losing sight of a *natural telos*, philology has yielded to "critical studies" incapable of freeing themselves from the shackles of utilitarian dictates, even and especially when scholars turn consciously to the business of constructing, in the medievalist Norman Kretzmann's all-too-modern words, "a sort of Grandest Unified Theory, with the capacity of being ultimately explanatory of absolutely everything."[20] Indeed, Kretzmann's universal aspirations do not free him in the least from the *tribal* principle for which he seeks confirmation in *his* Aquinas, whom Kretzmann conceives as reasoning/arguing to confirm his own beliefs *identified* with truth proper.[21] In sum, Kretzmann's Aquinas is but a steppingstone to be criticized and extended into a system that Kretzmann himself promised (himself) to deliver.[22]

Now, philology's contemporary predicament is unambiguously bound to the modern erring of philosophy away from its original mandate as contemplation of the *necessary* reason of things, entailing "meaningful order in nature" beyond any mechanical contingencies.[23] Given modern philosophy's abandonment of a classical, non-mechanistic conception of nature—a *Platonic* conception coherent with the free exercise human arbitration—late or post-modern scholarly debates over the question of divine creation have tended to rely upon philological reconstructions produced without explicit

## 8   Introduction

philosophical grounding.[24] Nature's indifference to art could not but translate into art's indifference to nature.

Today, philological research tends to be conducted as if it did not serve any properly philosophical end. Perhaps it doesn't. Yet, if it does not, then philosophy is being replaced by another guide, namely "historical consciousness" crystallized in the "historical method" of modern biblical criticism.[25]

Today's philology seeks rigor by relying upon a modern conception of science (*scientia*) that derives, in turn, from a peculiar conception of "natural philosophy" applied to human affairs. Spinoza, brilliant heir of Machiavelli (the Dutchman's *acutissimus* godfather), shows the way, inaugurating an age of "historical criticism" based on the modern assumption that the mind of God can be translated into what Descartes would name "clear and distinct ideas." How else could the "logic of History" be conceived, if not where mathematically discernible mechanisms, as opposed to the ultimately mysterious mind of God, were assumed to constitute the foundation of human life and order? Modern philology is not alien to such thoughts, even where it prefers to take them for granted, or where it pretends they are not there to sustain our "scientific" philology, allowing it to defend its prestige in the face of vulgar, "unscientific" discourse: remove Spinoza and the edifice of philosophical considerations he stood for, and contemporary philology falls at once, like a castle (not quite a cathedral) of cards. Yet, do philologists have a viable alternative to survive? What reason is available to them other than the "critical" one of modernity?

In the eighteenth century, Giambattista Vico answered our question by defending what he called a "poetic reason" (*ragione poetica*) allowing us to save philology from an impending disaster (Vico intimated unprecedented tyranny), which is what the twentieth century announced as "the destruction of reason," which carried within it two dramatic occurrences: the death of God and the crisis of civilization (arguably, no mere Spenglerian decline).[26]

That death and that crisis are poorly masked, today, by academic conformism, or the fiddling of intellectuals while Rome burns (to echo a Straussian locution), keeping in mind that the contemporary crisis brings with it the collapse of all traditional institutions, not least of them Academia.

This is not to say that our intellectuals are not aware of imminent threats to the ivory tower providing for the intellectuals' relative safety. They do notice, if only occasionally—for they could hardly avoid noticing—that Damocles's sword is no mere figment of an ancient, no longer relevant imagination. The trouble is that our academic experts are too busy attending to their philological "trees"—not to speak of daily overloads of bureaucratic fish to fry—to face the burning Forest and the post-philosophical dragon setting it on fire: *ideology*, or the rise of a mercenary discourse about reality cut off from reality, as of ideas cut off from truth proper.[27]

Philology *her*self begs for a hero ready to slay the dragon, thereby freeing Lady Philology from the grip of ideology. But where is the hero in our post-metaphysical age, in the age of God's death? Were God still "alive," philosophy could intervene to orient our philological acumen toward naturally enlightening vistas. Yet, God has been sentenced to death, leaving *human* providence devoid of formal support. What Vico called "poetic reason" is ostracized, in our age, in the name of a science that has, over the course of the past few centuries, converted into a technological Leviathan for which philology can be nothing more than a veneer for verbal manipulation, cardinal ingredient of the mass propaganda mediating our daily lives in the element of technology.

## Notes

1 Whitehead 1967.
2 If in discussing properties we are seeking knowledge or science, then we must assume that our properties are not merely conceptual tools we use pragmatically or expedientially to account for or deal with an otherwise unknowable reality.
3 The early-modern notion that some ideas are innate to things, whereas others are imposed upon things lends itself to equivocations that the present discussion seeks to undercut.
4 Cicero, *Epistles to Atticus*, 2.1.8.
5 This point is vividly highlighted in a humorous passage of *Paradiso* 1.67–69, where Dante alludes to the delusion of those who, having convinced themselves of having become divine, turn (so to speak) into fish under water.
6 On the meaning of "bravery" and "novelty" in the modern world, see my five articles on Shakespeare's *Julius Caesar* in *Voegelin View*, at https://voegelinview.com/author/marco-andreacchio/ (April 26–28, June 15 and 22, 2022).
7 For a discussion on Augustine's indebtedness to Varro, see p. 104 of Daly 1999.
8 Augustine's divine synthesis of nature and law responds to earlier poetry's failure, a failure that Augustine attributes to Varro even though it belonged more precisely to Rome's imperial elite and most notably Augustus, as Lundy 2015 punctually noted. Indeed, the "project" that is consonant with all that we have left of Varro's works is for poetry to *mediate* and *to some extent* harmonize nature and law, *lest* (not, so that) law (reason of State) resolve nature (natural reason) within itself. St. Augustine may then be said to share Varro's firm objection to tyranny in the form of the instrumentalizing of natural reason to *de facto* deify State authorities. Ironically, the Bishop of Hippo would be targeted *post mortem*, and most notably in the light of Constantine, as guilty of the very fault the Christian had imputed to the pagan Varro. Now, that fault would reemerge with vengeance in its vocal modern detractors who, having condemned the use of science or philosophy by "Christian" authorities seeking to subjugate the *demos*, opened the door to the terminal reduction of natural reason to the plaything of mercantile interests. How else could the modern rebellion against the *Ancien Régime* "solve" the problem of nature, or the conflict between masters and slaves (to speak with Hegel), if not by introducing a plutocratic parody of an older nominal or hollow aristocracy? (Lundy's argument becomes unconvincing where he begins projecting onto Varro the *modern* aspiration for a society founded on philosophy via the benevolent use of poetry; for that aspiration is radically incompatible with Varro's "antiquarian" interest in moderating, rather than satisfying popular sentiment.)
9 Augustine, *City of God*, Book 6.7.
10 See Andreacchio 2019.

10   *Introduction*

11 On the wide spectrum of senses of the term "ideology" (officially coined in France in 1796 by Antoine Destutt de Tracy), see Shiffman 2022.
12 Shelley 2008.
13 See Hobbes 1650, Chapter 9.13.
14 In Book. 10.5–7 of his *Confessions*, St. Augustine invites us to see that human knowledge and consciousness ("the inner man"/*homo interior*) are rooted in divine knowledge and consciousness as in their providential perfection, which is what is ultimately lovable about man, who alone among finite beings turns back single-mindedly (as "single mind"/*unus animus*) upon his perfection as root of all inner questioning (*interrogatio*), fulfillment of all desire. In this sense, in man alone (the "inner man" as unique life form) among all creatures does God know himself (in a determinate manner). Hence the radical intimacy of the relationship between man and God, as between life and "life's own life" (*vitae vita*). Hence also St. Augustine's *Platonic* testimony to our mind's ascent into God as "vast courtroom of my mind" (*aula ingens memoriae meae)*, or *grandis memoriae recessus* ("treasure"/*thesaurus* or "vast womb"/*ingens sinus*) consummate receptacle of our mind's "mnemonic" contents (8.xii-xiv). In this "infinitely vast recess of memory" (*memoriae . . . penetrale amplum et infinitum*—xv), "almost a cavern" (xvii), man discovers his unique destiny.
15 "*Alio modo dicimur aliquo iudicare de veritate aliqua, sicut virtute iudicativa; et hoc modo per intellectum agentem iudicamus de veritate*" (Aquinas, *De spiritualibus creaturis*, Art. 10, ad. 8). In reference to St. Augustine, Aquinas articulates his proposition further, admitting "the 'reasons' of things in the divine mind" (*rationes rerum in mente divina*) where, "thanks to them and according to an intellect illuminated by the divine light, we judge of all things" (*per eas secundum intellectum illustratum a luce divina de omnibus iudicamus—ibid.*). Our own intellect, in other words, would be illuminated by the divine intellect thanks to "ideas," where these "reasons" of things are gathered eternally in the divine intellect or mind. The "reasons" in question are that thanks to which things are and in being are intelligible to us "thanks to the light of the active intellect, which makes things intelligible" (*per lumen intellectus agentis, quod facit intelligibilia*). "Yet, little does it matter whether we say that it is the intelligible things themselves that are partaken in from God, or the light that makes intelligible things" (*non multum autem refert dicere, quod ipsa intelligibilia participentur a Deo, vel quod lumen faciens intelligibilia*). Why does Aquinas conclude his argument thus, if not because he sees it fit to caution us that the ideas of things (things in themselves) are ultimately none other than the light of divine intelligence?
16 Leo Strauss is arguably the most distinguished explorer of the essential genesis of nineteenth century rise of "History" and its correlative "historical consciousness." Strauss notoriously argued that historicism had obscured the classical tension between Reason/Athens and Revelation/Jerusalem, a tension that Strauss himself ostensively worked to highlight, most notably by reviving Maimonides as masterful guide to the heart of the tension in question and thus to a life bridging the two poles of Philosophy and Law. These problems are articulated anew in the present study in terms of the tension between nature and art *and* in a medieval Christian setting that received scant treatment in Strauss. Yet, the historicist challenge to the nature-art tension is only tangential to a study of medieval sources. By way of responding to that challenge, suffice to say here that no rigorous—both philologically and philosophically—reading of our medieval sources can rely on a mechanically super-imposed purported historical/cultural "context." Any such assumed context would stand as a hypothesis begging to be illuminated in the light of our sources, which is to say, our writers' arguments teleologically understood, or more precisely, by their *way of writing*. The writers would then rise as guides

to our understanding their context not as merely "historical," but Platonically as extending from the sensory to the purely intelligible. In sum, our sources' context is twofold, for it is at once nature (the fallen one of mortal beings) and eternal being (realm of death's redemption); likewise what will tie the Low and the High together is nothing other than our medieval discourse, their *human providence*, as opposed to any "laws," whether psychological ("subjective") or physical ("objective"), to which medieval, pre-historicist discourse would be unwittingly bound. No presumption will be made in favor of a context other than the twofold one that our sources readily recognized for their own work, indeed their own life. In this respect, Maurice Blondel's refutation of historicism is more convincing, because more thorough, than that of Karl Rahner. Compare Blondel 1904 and Rahner 1964. On Rahner's argument, our "historical" being unfolds without need for consciousness of divine providence (Grace), even though that providence must be at work in our daily life (135–39). Now, while this reading accords doctrinally with the notion of a pagan world oblivious the true God of biblical revelation, it does not take into account the intimate *actuality* of the work of grace at the heart of natural reason (Blondel's vindication of the dignity of "action" comes to mind). Granted that people may strive for infinite being without recognizing the immediate dependence of their striving upon an infinite being that would then be not only conceptually, but *existentially* relevant to the exercise of our freedom. But is awareness of the existence of the divine and so the sacred/theological gift of faith ever completely absent from natural reason and thus too classical, pre-Christian philosophy? Is consciousness of divine providence entirely obscured from classical pagan consciousness, as some Christians would want us to believe (asking rhetorically, "how could Plato ever conceive of God dying on a cross?"), or is it merely "submerged" by the rise of Christianity (if only assisted by the all-too-pious amanuenses who tore pages out of their copies of Cicero's *De natura deorum*—pages discussing the nature of divine providence) and only *thereafter* obscured entirely, as we enter into a post-Christian era? A pertinent consideration to tip the balance in Plato's favor: given the classical *poetic* character of natural reason, justice makes more practical sense than injustice (*pace* bold Thrasymachus). For kindred Thomistic considerations, see Torrell 2008: "Nature et grâce chez Thomas d'Aquin" (99–129; originally published in *Revue thomiste*, 101 [2001]: 167–202; hereafter *NG*), 126–27.
17 In Vico's words, philology is "the *Doctrine of all those things that depend upon human arbitration,* as are all the *Stories* of *Languages,* of *Customs* and of *Deeds* of *peoples,* both in peace and in war"—Vico 2013: 16.
18 See Langiulli 2000.
19 Scholars hoping to transcend the strictures of mechanistic conceptions of nature tend to ground their hope in little or nothing at all more than "antecedent sympathies," as we see in Nagel 2012. While Nagel readily acknowledges his lack of imagination, or his general incapacity to conceive of a nature rationally compatible with the phenomenon of consciousness, he takes his fault as a free-pass for a position espoused *mutatis mutandis* long ago by the Sophist Gorgias: even assuming there were a fundamental truth (viz., an original and necessary harmony between nature and human consciousness), we have no rational access to it ("it is perfectly possible" that this is the case "in virtue of our intrinsic cognitive limitations"; and in any case, we have no such access *today,* "at this stage in the history of science"—33). *Ergo,* all we can sensibly do *today* (and indeed all we are eminently justified in doing) is "generate and reject false hypotheses," given that "the human will to believe is inexhaustible" (128). Accordingly, while defending our "capacity to transcend the imperatives of biology" through/in reason, against mainstream reductionistic naturalists, Nagel bows unremittingly before the call "to understand consciousness as a biological phenomenon" (125 and 128). Where Nagel's "mind"

is *probably* irreducible to any *model* of nature, where no model is *likely* to ever fully account for nature as such, Nagel's skeptical (and not in Socrates's zetetic/teleological sense) defense of mind remains a rather shallow response to the supposedly "inexhaustible . . . human will to believe" (*ibid.*); as is Nagel's *de facto* replacement of natural teleology (at least partially obscured by Cartesian theism—31) with the historical "creation of new value" (124). In medieval terms, Nagel wants the Son without the Father: he defends the inherence of reason in nature, without the transcendence of reason with respect to nature as a whole. Nagel's transcendence is merely "local" (relative or qualified) so to speak, as he supposes our freedom to be, inevitably lost in history (32–33). But what if reason were originally nothing other than a bond between Son and Father, or between reason hidden in nature and reason revealed above it? What if Nagel's acknowledged incapacity to *radically* transcend the limits of contemporary naturalism (127) prevented him from discerning the *proper* nature of reason, or the essentially *teleological* character of mind? What if Nagel's concern with "models" of nature distracted him from the question of mind's original mandate, its *given* destiny? What if modernity's *homo faber* had blinded Nagel to the original and ultimate primacy of contemplation over any "building?"

20 Kretzmann 2001: 9. Kretzmann is an outstanding example of propounders of a "progressive" Aquinas as "contributor" to the universal "natural theology" of the future. See *ibid.*, 3–6. Kretzmann sees Aquinas as a model in the exercise of integrating "topics" introduced by revealed theology into a purely "philosophical" discourse that, however, can hardly be distinguished from a *historicist* discourse, keeping in mind that already in Hegel we have the loftiest consolidation of the modern ("Machiavellian") project of converting philosophy into ideology. *Contra* Kretzmann and the modern enterprise of intellectual history, the present work reads medieval scholars as disclosing a *poetic* landscape constituting a fundamental alternative to modern "History," in the act of mediating the natural and the divine. Accordingly, what is sought here is not the translation of divine "topics" into secular terms, but 1. the entering, or more precisely *ascending* of the human within the divine, or rather 2. the disclosure of the human as a "tendency" proper to the divine itself. That tendency would be none other than natural reason understood, not as an alternative to divine revelation, but as a free *predicate* of divine intellection. Necessarily, the reading articulated here will depart from any reading defined in the context of a progressive "building" of natural theology as secular system "providing support for religious beliefs," as William Alston (and Kretzmann after him) would put it, as if God were a *means* to better understand the variety of the "spheres" of human "experience." See Alston 1991: 289. Yet, perhaps Kretzmann would object that Aquinas reads natural reason as considering the nature of things as an end in itself, rather than for the sake of investigating the nature of God (cf. Kretzann's citing of *Summa contra Gentiles*, II.4.871)—as if Aquinas meant that the nature of things is a problem *aside from* that of the nature of *being itself*. To this possible objection, Aquinas could easily respond by citing Cicero's *De natura deorum* to show that, *pace* Kretzmann and Alston, natural theology does not aim at "providing support *for religious belief*" (Kretzmann 2001: 7*)*, but at investigating the nature of Gods, and so at mediating the hiddenness of the divine in nature and the revelation of the divine in law. It would follow that Aquinas's God is not that of modernity's "Intelligent Design theory," namely a God that we *use* to supply *a posteriori* meaning to our experience and indeed ultimately to "support" the plurality of our *secular* concerns. While Aquinas is overtly defending and thus confirming the Bible's authority against "natural philosophers" and by appealing to *political* ones such as Plato and Aristotle, "supporting beliefs" is not the proper aim what Aquinas recognizes for natural reason/philosophy. It is only *accidentally* that "reason" confirms "revelation" (*pace* Pierre Duhem, of whom more down the road of the present investigation).

21 *Ibid.*, 10–11.
22 *Ibid.*, 29. The system in question would have comprised a trilogy, had Kretzmann not died in 1998, shortly after publishing his tome on divine creation. Whereas the first tome (Kretzmann 1997) had been dedicated to the divine in itself, the third volume *would have been* dedicated to divine soteriology.
23 For our medieval authors, meaning or signification (*significatio*) coincides with intention (*intentio*): the meaning of something is necessarily teleologically configured towards intelligibility and is thus absolutely not any *ad hoc* (e.g., "sociohistorical") imposition/attribution. On the author's intention (*intentio auctoris*) for the late medieval scholarship, see Torrell 2008, "Saint Thomas et l'Histoire": "L'intention de l'auteur", 170–71. Evidently, scholars such as Thomas Aquinas would be prompt in reminding us that we could not know or think anything at all, but be merely lost in ever-mutating "sensations," in the absence of cognitive anchorage in immutable intelligence, whether this be presented in terms of separate Ideas, or as Ideas in God's own mind, as St. Augustine would insist, or of one uncreated, divine "active intellect" (*intellectus agens*, after Aristotle). Cf. Aquinas, *De spiritualibus creaturis*, Art. 10, ad. 8. The argument advanced by modern scholars such as Norris Clarke and Gregory Doolan that by placing the Ideas in God's mind, Aquinas would be clearly breaking from Platonism is blind to 1. Aquinas's own "intellectualist" argument for the primacy of spheres of intelligibility or of *fundamental questions* as absolute, irreducible birthplaces of things, over any nominal guarantor or overarching "answer," and 2. the "implicit" Platonic lesson that Ideas *are* in virtue of their common *being*, which must be one with intelligence itself, as Plato's Socrates suggested in praising Anaxagoras in *Phaedo* 97c1–2. The appeal to an overarching divine mind (νοῦς/*mens*) that contains the primordial forms of things, is by no means alien to Plato, who would arguably object, however, to a certain reading of the mind of God as something altogether other than the human mind. What is more, Platonically speaking, the "dependence" of the Ideas upon God's mind/thought should not be viewed in "personal" terms, as if there could be thought aside from Ideas. Aquinas himself, in defending a Platonic reading of Aristotle (whereby the "father" draws the "son" back to themself), reads the Stagirite as accepting Plato's doctrine of Ideas provided these forms be understood, beyond conventional appearances, as actively involved in, rather than alien and ultimately irrelevant to the constitution of our experience. Cf. Aquinas, *In Sent.*, Book I, Dist. 36, Q. 2, Art. 1. For Aquinas himself, what counts the most here is vindicating the *providential* immanence of the divine in the human, so that the *doctor angelicus*' appeal to the divine mind should not be construed as suggesting that the Ideas mark any deep rift between the human and divine. Clarke's distinction between "things themselves" and Ideas as "intentional similitudes" whose own being is nothing other than "one divine act of knowing" is not Aquinas's final word on the matter at hand (cf. p. 122 of Clarke 1982: 109–27). Not if Aquinas's God intervenes upon Ideas, not as a mere guarantor *ex machina*, but as *reflection* of what Ideas are in themselves—of their *being* as permanent forms of intelligibility. In this case, the multiplicity of ideas would not be *resolved*, but disclosed eternally by the unity of divine or perfect intellection. The appeal to God would then coincide with an appeal to the absolute irreducibility of the multiplicity of divine ideas and order—and so to the ultimate meaningfulness of human experience. Otherwise put, in Heaven our daily problems are not resolved, but disclosed as eminently good.
24 The "drama" of modern philology was denounced already by Vico in 1708 (cf. Vico 2022). While linking the problem in question to the influence of Descartes, Vico retraced the predicament of modern scholarship to the timeless problem of mutual alienation of reason and authority.
25 See Strauss 1949.

14  *Introduction*

26  On contemporary worldwide disenchantment vis-à-vis modernity's secularism, see Noé 2022. The collapse of the Modern Project (of transposing life onto a "virtual" platform) presaged most recently by the crash of the "crypto currency" market would have, evidently, colossal consequences for political order across the globe, plunging the nations of the world into a potentially terminal era of technologically-mediated barbarism by far more devastating than the one concomitant with the fourth and fifth centuries fall of the Western Roman Empire. For a recent ideologically informed attempt to "blame" the fall of Rome on discourse fueling rampant fear of foreign barbarians, see Watts 2021. Watts is misleading in presenting "traditional" accounts of the fall of Rome as demonizing foreign barbarians, since, as Vico's studies confirm, historians have long retraced Rome's fall to its internal/domestic degeneracy, one that (notwithstanding objections raised by Machiavelli and his ideological heirs) pre-dates and is ultimately incompatible with the rise of Christianity.

27  Leo Strauss retraced to Machiavelli the conversion of philosophy into ideology (see e.g., Strauss 1964: 2). Whereas philosophy proper stands for the indissoluble marriage of form and content/means/matter, ideology entails the mechanical application of nominalist symbolic abstractions to a "matter" conceived mechanically (as *res extensa*), or as generally devoid of intelligence. (Consider e.g., Barrow and Tipler 1986, where the authors, who hardly conceal their neo-Marxist leanings [203], go as far as to liken Aristotle's "form" (εἶδος/*eîdos*) to a "computer program" vis-à-vis a "physical computer" [680], while nailing Thomism to the cross of anti-scientific dogma [47–48]. Nor has the academic tide corrected its course since the 1980's.) The upshot of the "Machiavellian revolution" is the rejection of what Nicholas of Cusa would call "intellectual intuition" (*intuitio/visio intellectualis*—as in *De quaerendo Deum* ["On Seeking God"], 1.19) in favor of "points of view" governed, not by any divine mind, but by unconscious or subhuman forces at play in what the nineteenth century would invoke as "History" *singulare tantum*. Modernity's "ideology" pertains to the operationalizing of a "worldview" or *Weltanschauung* in which individual points of view (viz., those of Leibniz's monads) are gathered as collective, even archetypical (as per Jung) reflections of "the Spirit of an Age" (*Zeitgeist*). In this respect, philosophy is supposed to tell us more about philosophers than about reality per se. Hence the primacy accorded in our age to psychology over philosophy in reading human behavior and accounting for the reason why people say what they say. On Galileo's role in the "genesis" of our current state of affairs, see Husserl 1970: 23.

# 1 "Poetic Reason" as Key to Reading Medieval Authors

In his "Of Poetic Reason" (*Della ragion poetica*), first published in Naples in 1708, the political philosopher Gian Vincenzo Gravina defended the poetry of classical antiquity against its modern detractors, arguing that the former had served as mirror for awakening men to the truth of all things, whereas in later ages poetry had come to be seen as constructing a new world (or new worlds) opaque to any eternal verity.[1] In invoking "poetic reason," Gravina *de facto* vindicated a Renaissance Platonism that found its nemesis in the rise of a "new science" (Galileo's *nuova scienza*) aimed at establishing not merely verisimilitude or likely answers, but *the* true, in the guise of a final scientific account of all things, including thought itself, for which authors would begin conceiving a system.[2]

Writing a few decades after Gravina and taking his tacit cue from his predecessor, Giambattista Vico would produce a philosophical system exposing the constitutional epistemic and moral bankruptcy of modern scientific certainty, in favor of a classical Platonic-Ciceronian *poetic* philosophy or reason seen as naturally best suited to support Republics (political life and order) against the grain of all anarchic impulses. What was at stake, for Vico, was the perennial battle that, writing a century after Vico, Matthew Arnold would evoke in speaking of "Culture and Anarchy." Was truth naturally incompatible with law, as modern political theorists from Machiavelli to Spinoza and from Hobbes to Grotius had professed?[3] Did the thriving of Republics require an un-natural conception of and quest for truth and indeed the reinvention of truth as instrumental to the rise of a new Society making use of its new truth in the act of turning progressively away from an older conception of truth as metaphysically (unevolving) *given* (unconstructed) end in itself? In defense of natural reason, Vico argued that the public establishment of modern conceptions of science or knowledge was 1. based on a (nominalist) misreading of Christian/Medieval theology[4] and 2. fated to lead to the worse type of tyrannies, namely anarchy. The effect of the rise of modern science would be catastrophic, not because modern science would bring truth to bear upon a political order fundamentally incompatible with truth, but because modern science presupposed a "contractual" conception of the political—or a fundamentally a-political or "monastic" conception of man—making it impossible for truth and liberty to coexist without their being radically obscured, if only via their reconceptualization, whereby truth would be replaced by pretense and liberty by slavery. In the Machiavellian world that Shakespeare would define satirically as brave and new, virtue would be sought in raw power, while novelty and its daily shock-effect would overshadow all care for antiquity as provider of guidance in everyday moral-political affairs.

Whereas classical (both ancient and medieval) *poetic* reason had allowed for moderation in practical matters based on immoderation in thought, modern "scientific" reason resulted in (and was arguably constitutionally bound to) a moderating of thought leading *volens nolens* to immoderation in practical matters, under the evermore advertised assumption that what the philosophers of the past had intuited about the ultimate nature of things they had merely dreamed of. To speak crudely, their kingdom of heaven could be no more than a pie in the sky.

"The Moderns" (Vico's tone was no less skeptical than that of Vico's Irish contemporary, Jonathan Swift) would "critique" the theoretical immoderation of pre-modernity as being far too dangerous for political freedom. The "unverifiable" metaphysical "extravagances" of classical and especially medieval reasoning were seen as responsible for great political evils—not least of them what modernity eagerly condemns as wars of religion—or as damning traits of "dark ages," to borrow an expression Petrarch would coin in reference to the early centuries of the Middle Ages.

Vico responded that the sins of earlier ages were being magnified, nor redeemed by modern reason, which was *en route* to establishing truth as mere function of free-floating or self-validating certainty standing as a ticking bomb all too thinly veiling its vacuity by postponing inspection upon its own foundations to an asymptotic future that not even Hegel's "End of History" could incarnate.[5]

What did modern reason stand upon? One could not meaningfully say because, presumably, we could only make sense when speaking of what is clearly and distinctly illuminated by modern reason. Only the "surface" of things—the *quantifiable* appearance of things—could be reasoned about, so that the only life worth speaking of was one progressing away from death, as it were, a life where the limelight of worldly empowerment would obscure any light shining in the dark and thus too the reason that the Middle Ages had defended as natural.[6]

In a crucial sense, medieval scholarship was consciously tied to all that is obscure. Indeed, death and its mysteries stood at the top of the list of medieval rationalists' concerns. Beauty itself was seen in death, as medieval iconography suggests with striking eloquence, even though its concrete significance is far from self-evident to us heirs of a Romanticism whose "historical imitations" of the medieval mind are most unreliable, not to say misleading guides to dialogue with the prototypes (so much does C. S. Lewis's appeal to a medieval "discarded image" arguably confirm, if only unwittingly). For in Romanticism the death in which beauty is encountered is no seat of intelligibility, but a cesspool of demons, "symbols" of an unbridled imagination. And yet, Romanticism does at least expose a shortcoming of modern reason, if only by embracing as fate the *irrational* death that modern reason had otherwise sought to exorcise.

Medieval reason sees beauty in death by discerning *order*, not chaos in death. For a medieval, modern reason would be idolatrous, even blasphemous insofar as it demonizes death by cherishing life as something other than and negated by death, as a "paradise" devoid of unresolvable or permanent problems. For the medieval "poetic mind," on the other hand, paradise is not a place beyond problems (as Michelangelo's Sistine *Final Judgment* stands to remind us, after Dante), but a place where problems are exposed to pure intelligibility, or where problems are eternal springs of life and love. In death, the poet abides within problems, rather than being offended by problems, from without.

Poetry never ceased to vindicate order in death, but its voice grew fainter for people as they advanced into the consolidation of the modern "scientific" world, until poetry itself became by and large reduced to mere, even gratuitous fancy, incapable of bespeaking real or fundamental problems; problems underlying our everyday life experience; problems inherent in death itself. All but universally abolished, today, is the notion of "the poem"—and thereby, too, of comedy—as place of discovery of problems in which the poet does not only disappear, but live forever, though, again, not by fleeing death, but by seeing through it, as through beauty itself, to touch its "other side," a world in which death is one with life eternal.[7]

The death that the vulgar, the non-poet, shuns as but misery or loss, is recovery for the poet, even "recollection" (Platonically, *anamnesis*), a place in which life is gathered back to regain integrity beyond the "fracture" characteristic of our Fallen world. But poetry is dialogue, if only ultimately dialogue with and among the dead (as Dante suggests in the "Noble Castle" of his *Inferno*, Canto 4). Death is what the poet seeks beyond the hesitations, nay taboos of non-poets. For them, death and all reminders of it (from disease to uncontrolled or dangerous sexual intercourses) are horrid; for the unabashed, "radical" poet—as for Lucifer (the light-bearer *par excellence*), no less than for witches (*magi* as "wisemen") and medieval mystics—death is intimate encounter, communion, even blessed ecstasy, that *ex-stasis* in which man exits his inherently static or stale body (the *sōma* that for the Greeks is a *sēma*, or sign of death, namely a sepulcher), to become one, which is to say, to regain integrity.

Poetry allows for integrity in this (mortal) life, not as a mere dream or shadow cut off from reality or "the thing itself" (*res ipsa*), but as a sign that allows us to partake most concretely in eternal being beyond the reaches of the body; a sign in which, to echo the language of Eucharistic discourse, the eternal is present and alive in the temporal. Poetic integrity cannot be "proven" mathematically, but it can be *trusted* as the Orphic poet is by the savages he educates, as Dante (after Ovid) would promptly remind us.[8]

Trust is key, here, as the *fides* needed to supplement the mathematical-like proofs or experiments/experiences of natural reason. Both *ratio* and *fides* are required insofar as poetry is not merely mathematically, but *existentially* sound; for it can lead, not only angels hypothetically, but *politically* incarnate-souls, or intellect *meant to* descend into the dark to rise back into the light by bearing witness to the light in the darkest of hours. In this respect, reason without faith is vain, for it fails to recognize the twofold end of man, to speak with Thomas Aquinas, namely a reason animated faithfully or through poetic guidance ("the living word" of Platonic poets) by and back-to eternal being.[9]

In what sense is our end twofold? Through faith elicited by "inspired poets" we see in reason its own perfection as the *original* consummation of life itself. In or through poetry, reason is *alive* and thereby truly trustworthy; for poetry leads us to the inner chambers of reason, as opposed to abandoning us outside of reason's "Noble Castle" (as per Dante), left considering reason as a mere *datum* in the broader context of a Democritean Vortex. *Fides et ratio*, as Trust and Discourse, are both needed to fulfill our mandate as human beings for whom death is neither a mere hypothesis, nor a *factum brutum* of experience altogether opaque to reason. Trust in God via trust in the poet as "earthly father" (again, to speak with Dante) draws us to the interiority of a natural reason that is no longer mistaken as providing a "merely-philosophical" truth; for now natural reason is seen as a mirror in which eternal being itself shows itself in the darkness of our Fallen world, not, to be sure, so as to seduce us, as Circe would, into remaining in this Valley of Tears we call World, but so as to call us out of it—as the Jesus of John 15:19 tells us when announcing, "I call you out of this world," adding at once, "and that is why the world hates you" (*ego elegi vos de mundo propterea odit vos mundus*). Διὰ τοῦτο, reads the Greek, indicating that the world has an evil or satanic gravitational pull on us, a "weight" (*gravitas*) that is countered by the living word "choosing" us as signs of what transcends this world (ὁ κόσμος). We would then not be intended to merely populate or decorate this world, but to testify to its inadequacies, by reminding *each other* of a Paradise Lost. Of paramount importance, here, is the dialogical character of the reminder: the *logos* that lives among men is *dia-logos*, just as the death we enjoy in this world we meet lovingly in the eyes of the Other, most dangerously. And "for this" (*propterea*), the Fallen world, the world fallen from the poetic or intimate life of souls, "hates you" (μισεῖ ὑμᾶς ὁ κόσμος, to return to John 15:19). Misanthropy, as Plato had reminded us, follows directly from misology, the hate of natural reason, of the reason of political beings and thus of a *logos* exercised among us, as we remind each other of death and in that reminder *live* death, "preparing" for it by *rehearsing* it. And this is the essence of art ("maieutic," says Plato's Socrates) as *imitatio naturæ*, the "imitation" of a nature that, far from being a mere machine to be reproduced mechanically, is a generative act to be lived artistically, as we rehearse generation by opening it up to its eternal prototype, namely a discourse/*logos* from One to One, or, to hearken to the doctrine of the Trinity, from Father to Son—the Father "in action"—and back, everlastingly.[10]

The twofold life of man, the life of both Faith and Reason, of both Jerusalem and Athens, whereby "faith seeks intellection" (*fides quaerens intellegere*, as per Anselm's *Proslogion*) confirms the cardinal role of man in the constitution of a nature that is not a "merely-material" substratum for expendable spiritual pursuits, but a potentiality begging for man's exposure of its original actuality, as of nature's own Nature, to speak with Jacob Klein.[11] Man is that "center" in which nature reflects its divine, originative being. "And that is why" those who are lost in nature by mistaking the fractured (*natura corrupta*) for the integral (*natura integra*),[12] or the currently-normal ("the conventional") for the natural *simpliciter*, hate both poetry and poets. For these "haters" reject the center, the cardinal, *heroic* role of man in the constitution of nature, swearing by a nature that swirls endlessly in an ultimately irrational frenzy.

Our end is twofold insofar as we are here 1. as men to mirror the divine *and* 2. as the divine that mirrors itself in us, as Christ lives in St. Paul in *Galatians* 2:20. We are here *politically* as inhabitants of St. Augustine's *City of God*, but we are here also *theologically*, mandated by and for eternal being. Twofold is then the end or happiness of a man who is at once political and theological, or theological *through* his political-poetic agency; of a man who is humanized as he gives himself to the divine; of a man who becomes himself or one and transcends his obstacles or fractures by rendering his entire life, his powers, to their creative source.

## Notes

1 In Gravina 2005. Gravina's argument, no less than Vico's kindred one, was directed only tangentially against medieval "proto-modern" conceptions of divine grace as subverting, rather than vindicating nature. For a representative anti-Platonic reading of classical-medieval conceptions of physical nature (incl. Aristotle's and Aquinas's) as anticipators of modern chemistry, see Bittle 1946.

2 As Jacob Klein aptly noted, the notion of any system of thought (of a system in which thought could define itself once and for all and thereby convert into an "objective means") is essentially modern; as is the notion of a "history of thought" of which we are to seek a "logic" mechanically *ready-at-hand*, rather than the *thought* within which the "history" unfolds *dialogically* in terms of surface-modifications of an underlying human mind. On the overt primacy of concern for likelihood over concern for "scientifically conclusive" formulas in Maimonides, see Manekin 1990: 117–41. As Andrew Gluck suggested, if only by framing his point in modernist terms, Maimonides shows considerably more concern for people losing faith in divine Law, than for people being led astray from truth proper (Gluck 1998: 249). More broadly speaking, medieval scholarship tends to adhere to the ancient view (intimately rejected by modernists or progressives such as Voltaire) that we should worry more about the threat of religious anarchy than about that of superstition

*even as* philosophy should never be debased into supporting either or both (*viz.*, via the advocacy of a "religion of Reason" in which enlightenment and obscurantism come to coincide). The problem of thought being trapped in its own universe is cardinal in Dante's *Comedy*, where the poet "descends" into the dark recesses of mind only to discover (or help the reader discover) that the descent can be converted into an ascent consummated in an awakening to the metaphysical nature of mind.

3 For a more thorough treatment of Vico's response to the most renowned early-modern political theorists, see Andreacchio 2013.
4 See Rahner 1964: 118–19.
5 In following Kant's arguments, one gathers the impression that the dispassionate examination of the foundations of modern freedom might be the ultimate act of impiety. On the tension between medieval and modern discourse (including Hegel and Kant), see Andreacchio Spring/Summer, 2019.
6 On the modern abstraction of a "realm of quantity" out of the reality attended to by classical-medieval people ("East and West"), see Guénon 1972.
7 The present work is the first, to its author's knowledge, to vindicate or recover the original poetic import of Latin medieval scholarship in the aftermath of the eclipse of classical-medieval "poetic reason" carried out most notably by the nineteenth century "historical criticism" established in German universities in the wake of Spinoza. Hibbs 1995 offers an example of "distractions" from the medieval art of writing, promising the read Aquinas's work as "divine comedy," while in fact reading comedy, not via Dante (not one reference to the Florentine), but *historicistically* via the likes of Eric Auerbach, Northrop Frye, René Girard and Paul Ricoeur (see esp. 171–77). A pity, given Hibbs's otherwise happy suggestion that Aquinas's work deserves to be read with an eye to its "dialectic and narrative." (Did Hibbs forget that truth hides always in nature's dangerous waters, as Dante saw well upon entering into "wild wilderness" or *la selva selvaggia*; cf. *Inferno* 1.5).
8 Dante, *Convivio*, II.1.ii-iv.
9 Bradley 1997 sought the soul of Aquinas's work in a faith beyond reason, rather than as faith at the heart of reason, or as Plato's poetic impulse at the heart of Aristotle.
10 In Book 13.11 of his *Confessions*, St. Augustine invites us to see creation as depending upon God's essential "trinitarian" articulation in terms of being, knowing, willing (*esse, nosse, velle*): for God *is* and in being *knows* and in knowing *wills* in the respect that he leads/gathers the known into being/unity. God then unifies/creates in knowing, or in illuminating. Otherwise put, he unifies intellectively. Herein is the heart of "participation" in God, for in being-made-one we partake in intelligible being. Hence Augustine's proclamation: "in your illumination we shall see illumination" (*in lumine tuo videbimus lumen*—16). In God's own understanding we shall understand (or "renew our minds"—22), just as in his being we shall be, while in his cognitive-gathering (which is what God's judging consists in—23) we shall gather our own identity; wherein do we find the basis for Augustine's advise to his reader, in light of Matthew 19: "to follow God, if you want to be perfect" (*sequere Dominum, si vis esse perfectus*—19) and thereby "shine" as a light in the firmament. So that in that light others may recognize the inherence of divine agency in the constitution of every finite being, through which alone anything can be good or complete (13.30–13).
11 See Klein 1985.
12 *ST*, I, 2, Q. 109, Art. 2. Aquinas's argument invites an inspiring thought: in his pre-corrupted state, man/Adam does not have to face challenges that are likely to render him more keenly, or simply reflectively aware, in his fallen state, of the active presence of divine agency in human agency. In this respect, it might be through the Fall alone that Adam comes to face himself, if only in the element of reflection or in the mirror of an unachievable paradigm, as Christ (Second Adam).

# 2 Theology or Philosophy? A False Dilemma

The foregoing considerations invite a breakthrough in the war between theology and philosophy, without seeking to reduce either to the other, or confuse the two terms by way of advancing the cause of some discipline or another along the lines of "intellectual history." The obvious deserves to be stated at once: philosophy is naturally theological, or open to the divine. The critical question, here, is whether or not natural reason is properly "unaided" and thus, somehow, autonomous of divine intervention, not to speak of physical compulsions, not least of them the fearsome bolt of lightning that brutes recognize as their first and fiercest God. Now, on a traditional Christian reading, natural theology (philosophy properly understood, or our free desire open to the infinite perfection of being) cannot resolve within itself divine intervention, or *revealed* theology. Likewise, the *being* of God does not require (even less does it account for) God's *existence*. Divine *necessity* does not self-evidently imply divine *freedom*. Natural reason would then seem to concern itself only with the necessity of God, rather than with God's existence, or concrete providence in the exercise of natural reason itself. The God of philosophical or natural theologians is *gnōsis gnōseos* (γνῶσις γνώσεως) or *noēsis noēseōs* (νόησις νοήσεως), as Aristotle showed, "thought thinking itself," rather than the love proclaimed by Scripture. And yet, on this view, philosophy is resolved in its own surface, its *opinions*, as if philosophy were alien to the "depth of implications" and even "the sublime insights" that Karl Rahner would readily concede to be hidden within "the truth expressly stated" by Christian theology.[1] But what if philosophy were truly at home in the sublime depth of its pronouncements, its "formulas of words?"[2] What if mysticism were a philosophical category prior to its becoming, on a modern reading, the prerogative of post-philosophical theologians? Then the real divide would not be between natural reason and divine intellect, but between natural reason conceived extrinsically or superficially (exoterically, one might say) and natural reason *lived* from within. Then we could meaningfully say that philosophy is above all a maturing of awareness or consciousness not merely *about* God, but *out of* God, whereby the philosopher disappears to himself as St. Paul would in Galatians 2:20 before the Christ of whom he swears to be the Apostle. But is

DOI: 10.4324/9781003405689-3

St. Paul not treading here in the footsteps of a pagan Greek philosopher who had sworn to be unwittingly (*malgré lui*, might interject Molière) mandated by Apollo? As the "apostle" of Apollo, Socrates was so self-forgetful as to lend himself, not only to be mocked in Aristophanes's *Clouds*, but also to be portrayed as mystic and saint by Stoics all the way into the Italian Renaissance.³

When all is said and done, or where all men stand "apocalyptically" outside of conventional conceptual compartments, Socratic arguments emerge as mere, even ironic signs of the inner chambers of the Socratic mind. What is hidden there cannot be "proven" or "experienced" the way the dwellers of Plato's Cave would be compelled to do; for the light or life of the mind can never be grasped by the flesh, that dark principle that the ancients shunned as turning the body (σῶμα/*sōma*) into the mind's own tomb (Romans 8:13 and John 1:5). And yet, the discourse of classical antiquity mediated what is naturally hidden and what is conventionally prominent. The two poles were maintained in creative tension as long as discourse did not abandon its *poetic* character to leap to a "scientific" solution in which the hidden would be universally exposed, or in which the revelation of the depths of the mind would be altogether worldly, or secular. A perfect recipe for obscurantism.⁴

## Notes

1 Rahner 1964: 114–15.
2 In *Convivio* IV.30.vi, Dante would speak of "Philosophy . . . whose proper reason is hidden in the most secret recesses of the divine mind!" (*Filosofia . . . la cui propia ragione è nel secretissimo della divina mente!*). A proposition that reads today as a warning, at once gentle and austere, not to try to understand medieval philosophy aside from its proper, "pre-historical" context.
3 A vivid testament of the saintly status that Socrates enjoyed in the Renaissance is still visible in the floor mosaics of the Siena Duomo.
4 See Andreacchio, Sept. 23, 2022.

# 3 A Universe from Nothing beyond Theology?

In his "Afterword" to Lawrence Krauss's *A Universe from Nothing*, Richard Dawkins argues that contemporary "science" has delivered a "knockout blow" to theology by having reached the daunting and apparently mathematically verifiable conclusion that the universe comes from nothing, teaching that we have abundant "evidence" to support the thesis, unlike "theologians" who merely (read, foolishly) speculate (read, dream) about the most bizarre things. This is not to say that our new scientists do not admit that what they teach is any less "weird" or any more "comprehensible than any theology"; quite to the contrary. The watershed between what "science" says and what "theology" says is marked by science's "work": "but science works. It gets results."[1] Thus spoke Dawkins, apparently without noticing in the least how his discourse sounds like a distorted echo of Christian theological sermons. Has Christianity not long warned against those who believe they could justify their assertions based on their "works," or "what works?" We deliver results, asserts the apologist of a *new* science that speaks "as if" it stemmed from nothing, as its own universe. For it more or less tacitly rejects any notion of a pre-modern science. No question of a reason naturally or necessarily open to the divine.

Dawkins' reason belongs strictly to a post-theological, mechanistic universe where all that counts can be "counted"—as the lunatics of Saint-Exupéry's *Petit Prince* would surely agree. The watershed between reality and illusion is marked by "counting." Counting makes our dreams "work" and as they work they can be trusted above all dreams that do not *stricto sensu* "work." Not a word, however, not a question about what is meant, here, by "work" or "results." In all endeavors we have trade-offs; we sacrifice X to obtain Y. Hierarchically, we must give up childish concerns in order to attend to manly ones (1 Corinthians 13:11). So what sacrifice does modern science involve? To begin with, blindness to a pre-modern understanding of "what works." Traveling to Venus (Dawkins' own example) does *not* work for someone wishing to keep his feet one Earth. Nor does "a theory that predicts the real world" work for someone understanding "the real" as fundamentally unpredictable, or predictable only locally and at the dire price of our blinding ourselves to the integrity of reality and so to the inalienable bond between what can and what cannot be predicted. But then Dawkins, after Krauss, warns us that reality is extremely "unstable" and that this instability is *the* key to understanding "why" something comes out of nothing. "Nothingness" is extremely unstable. Yet, change the name and what our new scientists have is *mutatis mutandis* a rather fidgety God. A God whose sole attribute is instability and so *unreliability*; a God of whom we can ultimately predict only one thing, namely that he or it will not stay put for long in his own "nothingness," but will be compelled by his own compulsive nature to blurt out "something" out of his "nothingness." As incoherent people are all apt to do.

Our "works" or what "works" for us *today* is supposed to justify the modern doctrine of creation from nothing over and above its medieval predecessor. But what is it that "works" for us, today? The "great discoveries of the twentieth and twenty-first centuries" about "the reality that lies hidden until we are brave enough to search for it." And "that is why"—according to Krauss—"philosophy and theology are ultimately incapable of addressing by themselves the truly fundamental questions that perplex us about our existence." For, "until we open our eyes and let nature call the shots, we are bound to wallow in myopia" (*ibid.* 178).

Krauss appears to have used certain "works" to blind himself to *the* fundamental questions that he has come to misconstrue in terms of questions defined by what he searches to begin with. Indeed, Krauss writes as if the modern physicist were listening to nature's own voice, as opposed to distorting that voice by abstracting quantifiable data from it and then projecting that data back onto nature as a whole—as if our data were representative of nature as a whole, or of the Nature of nature.[2] What greater fallacy, what worse myopia than the one involving mistaking a model of predictions for reality as a whole? Even a novice is natural reasoning can readily discern that our predictions are always tied to certain expectations and interests—indeed, to our very formulations—or that every prediction is "local" or "relative" (Krauss concedes this latter point, but he infers that the relative is all we have, given that what is beyond relativity is declaratively "nothing").

What *classical* science cares about is not predicting, but rising to what is *always:* eternal being. Return, rather than progress. For eternal being cannot, strictly speaking, be predicted, even as it can be mysteriously divined. The classical prophet speaks of things hidden, not "physically," but ontologically; he speaks of a world of intelligibility, a "spiritual" plenitude presupposed by the brokenness or fallenness of nature, the turmoil of circumstances that we otherwise experience daily.

Post-philosophical writers such as the "physicist" Krauss have forsaken (and incite us to do likewise) the plenitude of nature for mechanically abstracted aspects of nature, because in doing so they can "predict" (for us?) and make things "work" (for them?) and have quantifiable "results" (for everyone?), thereby confirming everyone as Hobbesian *homines fabri*, men born to "build" rather than to use what is built as a mirror for contemplation of that which Is without ever having been made.[3]

The propagandistic rhetoric of modernists, or rather trans-modernists,[4] of the caliber of Krauss and Dawkins is strategically silent about its own ground and thus 1. about modern science being essentially a sub-species of philosophy and 2. about theology being the heart of philosophy/science even where "revealed theology" rises authoritatively to provide "existential" confirmation of the verities proclaimed by "natural theology." In a classical-medieval sense, theology is none other than *naturally and divinely rooted reason*, so that what its contemporary academic detractors stand for it not reason *simpliciter*, but a "historical" deformation of natural reason, a deformation that blinds us to the non-evolutionary character of natural reason, ostensibly in the name of "nothing," or for the sake of establishing a theology without *logos*, or a divine-like authority without reason. But authority without reason, or authority opaque to its roots is indistinguishable from tyranny, or the replacement of authority with violence.

Unsurprisingly, violent is the anti-poetic rhetoric of propagandists such as Dawkins, whose appeal to universal enlightenment and "real answers" silences, at times with sneering sarcasm, at times with virulent *ad hominem* attacks, any question that does not docilely fit in a Cartesian grid. Until the dividing line between science and ideology is entirely erased and the totalistic vision of the insurgent science comes to coincide with the rise of a totalistic society whose foremost imperative is the abolishment of "the inner life."[5]

How, in sum, are we to account for the substance of today's anti-theological arguments? Their "universe from nothing" carries within it one terminal message: the triumph of imperfection over perfection. Utterly rejected, even denigrated, is the classical and medieval notion that perfection is implied by imperfection as the latter's original *actuality*.[6] Against this commonsensical view, today's anti-theological ideologue recycles old Christian spiritualist/Gnostic heresies to assert that the imperfect is fundamentally imperfect or flawed. Is there an original Good or blessing, or are we, including our reason, ineluctably lost in "nature?" The anti-theological ideologue takes pride in his "bleak" answer, which he "bravely" projects upon nature itself (Dawkins, in Krauss 2012). The challenge of entering into dialogue with classical-medieval authors undermines the sense of self-accomplishment or satisfaction of contemporary ideologues, inviting us to shed their reductionist blinders for the sake or exposing ourselves (anew) to a "nothingness" that promises to be as pregnant with meaning, with intelligibility, as death itself is for pre-modern civilization.

It is not mere disenchantment with modernity that sustains our turn to pre-modern authors, as much as we may agree that, rather than inaugurating an age of universal liberty, modern "naturalistic" reductionism has fostered an atheistic or religious anarchy converting at once into ideological despotism. A *positive* impulse sustains our "turn," an impulse that is more realistically positive than a "progressive" science blind to any permanent grounds for distinguishing science from sheer ideology.[7]

The appeal to a medieval alternative to modern rationalism invites recognition of a *fallacy of reification* whereby empirical determinations of thought are mistaken for sources of thought, as if thought or consciousness could be produced simply by its unconscious absence. The modern notion (relentlessly dissected by Edmund Husserl) that "the animate" or consciousness can be produced *ex nihilo*, that it "evolves" directly from the inanimate or the unconscious, is mirrored by the notion that the context or outer-form of experience is defined by some content or another of experience and thus by a determination of consciousness. Not only human consciousness, but also divine consciousness will then be reduced *materialistically* to the unconscious. But on what grounds?

In taking refuge in its own makings, modern man seeks respite from the dangers that his predecessors had long remained exposed to. The classical and medieval metaphysics abhorred by the founders of modernity (Kant is here most emblematic) is a dangerous enterprise teaching moderation of the body via heroic immoderation in a thought that does not shy away from recognizing itself as rooted in a supra- or meta-empirical context of experience. The immoderation ostensively abhorred by the ideological-scientific progeny of Machiavelli is one that interprets the contents of experience as oneiric-like, *poetic* signs of the creative meta-empirical context of experience.

What is wrong with the classical fashioning of poetic accounts of the metaphysical limits of experience? Such accounts would clash against all tendencies to identify the "dangerous" limits of experience with any determinate content of experience, whereby truth would be implicitly redefined as safety. Classical metaphysics would have questioned any finite limits of our experience in favor of discovering an infinite or unbound limit that alone would allow for the conservation of political/human life and order by supporting with constant moderation indeed against all barbaric compulsions, or that anarchic wind of madness that Matthew Arnold would boldly juxtapose to "culture" *singulare tantum*. All finite limits of experience, for classical metaphysics, are *poetic challenges*, rather than "scientific laws" for our experience: they signify a divine "experience" or "experiment," permanent content of an eternal consciousness. Accordingly, for pre-modern man we have no access to a "scientifically true" or "most certain" (*certissimus*) account of experience, but to poetically, commonsensically-*likely* accounts (not *the* true one, but various true ones) that are sound insofar as they help us expose ourselves to the *indefinite*, absolute limits of our experience. The pre-modern challenge is not 1. to construct a best or perfect "model" of reality, one that can account for and thus somehow predict all empirical variations—or the way the present disappears into the past—but 2. to *imitate* our ordinary experience in "artistic creations" serving as mirror-stages of reflective-dialogue in which we expose ourselves, the entirety of our conscious life, to our divine perfection, absolute boundary of all possible finite experience.

## Notes

1 Krauss 2012: 187–91.
2 Klein 1985, "On the Nature of Nature": 219–39.
3 Thomas Aquinas has by no means been spared the "honor" of being inscribed within a modernist *Weltanschauung*. See Torrell 2008, "Saint Thomas et l'Histoire," 172–75. Torrell's text includes references to various attempts, approved of by Torrell himself, to read Aquinas as a proto-historicist. A single suggestive objection calls to be raised here in response to a certain contemporary trend to modernize the medieval scholar: Aquinas did not set out to build any System (be it named philosophical, theological, or historical), but to integrate the "voices" resounding throughout the ultimately *synchronic* (mystical/poetic) "landscape" of all discernible ages into a *dialogue* (Oakeshott's "Conversation of Mankind" comes to mind, here) reflecting divine intelligence at the heart of human life. The *doctor's summae* ought to be understood, not as precursors of any "theology of history" (Torrell, 174), but *mediating* (whence their essentially "poetic" character) the human/political/ethical and the divine/metaphysical, though not in the service of any "historical consciousness." Nothing is more alien to the project of upholding "the intrinsic historicity of the human reality" (*l'historicité intrinsèque de la réalité humaine—ibid.*) than Aquinas's vindication of essential (both ontological and epistemic) continuity between human reason and divine intelligence. The fact that Aquinas testifies to that continuity dialogically confirms, rather than undermine the altogether meta-historical task of medieval *Platonic* scholarship: to respond to the eternal by ordering the temporal in its light. (For further reflections on a classical-medieval conception of "time" coherent with Aquinas's work, see Andreacchio, Feb. 2, 2022).
4 See earlier explanation of my neologism.
5 See Andreacchio, Jan. 6, 2021. For a classical statement on the primacy of perfection within imperfection, see Augustine, *Confessions*, Book 13.4.v.
6 The medieval warning against the "Aristotelian" thesis that the universe is eternal and as such not needing any reference to God to explain *itself*, points in the direction of the fundamental moral and epistemic bankruptcy of "scientists" such as Krauss and Dawkins. Their radical immanentism is a sepulcher they have leaped into, if only to hide from a truth hiding in transcendent danger. On immanentism as mind numbing trap to be avoided by recurring to the *medieval* doctrine of "creation from nothing," see Maimonides, *Guide of the Perplexed* (hereafter *Guide*), 2.25, where the doctrine helps sustain the creative tension between philosophical questioning and the religious certainties that constitute the formal bedrock of political life and order. Yet, the thesis that the universe/world is eternal can be understood to be incompatible with revelation, not in itself, but in the minds of most men, or superficially. Gluck 1998 does not consider this possibility, concluding that the thesis in question undermines the Torah *fundamentally* (250 and 252).
7 A fuller introductory articulation of the distinctions under consideration is found in Hilail Gildin's "Introduction" to Strauss 1989: vv-xxiv.

# 4 Medieval Scholarship as Guide in Interpretation?

The seventeenth century is replete with mockeries of medieval reasoning and logic, highlighting their dogmatic, not to say obscurantist character. What modern scholarship does not always recognize is that medieval scholarship disposes of medieval corruption with unsurpassed acumen. From St. Paul's deprecation of false eloquence, passing through St. Augustine's condemnation of our *libido dominandi*, or even the goliardic verses of *Carmina Burana*, all the way to Dante's assault on scholastic "blackbirds," medieval Christianity proves not to be alien to enlightening vindications of natural reason in the face of an impostor that does not perfect, but destroy nature, or natural sentiment; unlike the divine providence that Thomas Aquinas invokes when swearing that *gratia non tollit naturam, sed perficit*: divine intellection does not rend our nature, but fulfills it.[1]

When it comes to defending natural reason and thus too philosophy, medieval Christians did not shy away from asking the most difficult questions, reaching out to the very first of all questions, namely that of the nature of being itself: of 1. the perfection of being, as well as of 2. all that falls short of that perfection, which is to say the universe or complete order of finite/determined beings. How is the universe of finite beings derived from the infinite perfection of being-itself? How are the two poles mediated? What is the nature of that which mediates perfect being and imperfect beings? In what way, if any, is perfection inherent in imperfection? Can perfect being save reason from falling prey to unreason, allowing us to plunge into imperfection without drowning into its ocean, rising instead back to the surface of our Platonic Cave, to see the light and live in it? Finally, is divine intellection—the thought or consciousness of perfect being—actually present in human reason, or the effort of finite beings to return to a long lost perfection, as to that which alone could ever complete them, their desire?[2]

To take seriously authors such as Boethius, Aquinas and Peter Lombard (celebrated "Master of Decrees" or *magister sententiarum*) is impossible without taking seriously God's own presence among men, thereby taking seriously both divine and human providence. Only then can our philological study be guided in the spirit of truth (through *fides*),[3] beyond the strictures of any "hermeneutics of suspicion," by a reason open to pure intelligibility—a reason that, on account of Aquinas's Platonic tradition, arises in the shadow of perfect intelligence (*ratio oritor in umbra intelligentiae*).[4] Such a reason would be, in turn, ready to see in philology a provider of certainties reflecting nothing less than truth itself—certainties confirming, as Vico would insist, philosophy as love of wisdom.

Let Reason (Philosophy) be open to divine intelligibility; Philology will be able to rely on Philosophy's heroic intervention to slay the Nemean Lion and restore the peace that philologists require to attend to their "trees" without falling prey to anxiety. Philologists need not attend to the Forest, as such, but they must allow Philosophy—that old metaphysical *ancilla socratica* who does not shy away from her capital "P"—to place philological certainties in the service of pure intelligibility, or more precisely of a human responsive-ascent to thought unbound.[5] Must, it is said, lest philology fall into the hands of ideology, speech trading the eternal for a Tower of flesh, a "Global Order" that we are summoned to build collectively as its own and sole guarantor.

## Notes

1 *ST*, I. Q. 1, Art. 8, ad. 2. See further Torrell 1996: 301–02.
2 St. Augustine presents out common yearning as sign of the original inherence of the human in the divine. Our common "remembrance of the happy life" (*vitae beatae recordatio*—10.21) would suggest that God is none other than active or providential truth at the bottom of our own mnemonic consciousness (23–25). In light of his "reminder," Augustine explores or rather warns against the multiplicity of distractions from truth, including "curiosity" (*curiositas*—35), ordinarily fueling the compulsive establishment of man as alternative to God (38). It is by way of countering fallen man's drive to forget God that Augustine invokes Jesus Christ as mediator between God and man, as he in whom paradigmatically man turns back to the divine perfection of his own being (43).
3 Consider Augustine's *Confessions*, Book. 13.6–7, where the divine spirit (*Spiritus Dei*) is the "spreading" of God's Word over the dark, to gather beings into their perfection, or the "place" (*locum*) in which they are complete (9); keeping in mind that aside from the generative "gathering" in question, no finite being could ever arise in the first place (10).
4 *In Sent.*, Book 2, Dist. 3, q. 1, sc, citing as authority the Platonist Isaac ben Solomon Israeli (cf. Israeli's *Liber de definitionibus*). The "definition" reappears in Albertus Magnus, *Super Dionysium De divinis nominibus*, 7.17. For an overview of the significance of Israeli's work for Aquinas, see Matula 2012: 239–46.
5 On the sharp incompatibility between modern rationalism (methodologically materialistic or atheistic) and Aquinas's appeal to reason as participation in divine intellection, see Jolivet 1935, esp. Ch. 1 (69–80).

# 5 Aristotle or Plato? Another False Dilemma

The study of medieval scholarship has long been marked by a tension between two formidable landmarks on our civilization's intellectual landscape: Aristotle and Plato. What *problems* underpin the distinction, if not outright opposition between these two *names*?[1] To speak with explicit reference to medieval discourse, "Plato" represents the "essential" bond between the human and the divine, whereas Aristotle represents their "genetic" distance. Accordingly, the Platonist will *formally* stand for the *immediacy* of intellective perfection as eternal context of and archetypal solution to all onto-epistemic imperfection. On the other hand, "Aristotle" will *formally* represent *mediation* (and thus too a need for moderation) between eternal perfection and temporal imperfection. Accordingly, the medieval schoolman will face the challenge of integrating both Plato and Aristotle into a single *sermo*, or coherent discourse. Occasionally, discussions will emphasize eternal prototypes over their temporal instantiations; but then the latter always return as practical points of departure for a methodic ascent to immutable paradigms,[2] with the understanding that the *end* given by nature or God never renders expendable the task of accounting for the abyss separating the Light of Being and the darkness alluded to apocalyptically in John 1:5.

Why then would modern scholarship, with few notable exceptions (from Nietzsche and Heidegger to R. J. Henle and Lloyd P. Gerson and passing tangentially through Leo Strauss),[3] have tended to read post-patristic medieval scholarship as primarily Aristotelian? The superficial answer is in plain view: late-medieval universities were pervaded by reverential appeals to Aristotle, whom Dante would aptly designate as "the teacher of the wise" (*'l maestro di color che sanno—Inferno* 4.131). What modern scholarship tends to downplay, if not altogether ignore, is that the medieval adaptation of Aristotle to the Bible was made possible in a *Platonic* "rhetorical" context. That *poetic* context, rather than any doctrinal framework, was the one Aristotle himself worked within as he sought to respond to contemporary detractors of philosophy as Way of Life.

Aside from Thomas Aquinas's blatant misreading of Plato (the one we usually "excuse" considering that the Neapolitan had no access to most of the

Greek's dialogues), there is nothing seriously un-Platonic about the medieval scholar. Nothing at all, as the present study should show *en passant*. Why, upon reflection it should become evident that Plato or a Platonic "intellectual intuition" animates the entirety of Aquinas's discourse (and is thus not merely topical as Cornelio Fabro would suggest almost a century ago, exploring the notion of "participation" in the *doctor angelicus*),[4] refuting all modern attempts to inscribe that discourse in a context other that the originally intended one, namely the twofold one of nature and God.[5]

What most, if not perhaps all modern readers have forgotten, avoided or failed to take seriously is 1. the "pre-modern" character of Aquinas's discourse *and* 2. the way our own modern "Cartesian" upbringing is likely to shape our hermeneutics. What in the present study is sought is neither a Platonic doctrine imported into the Thomistic text, nor one deduced out of it,[6] but *participation* in the poetic/dialogical context of our sources. Participation not as a fossilized doctrine, but as a living engagement of which there can be no "extrinsic" proof or experience. For that engagement is and is lived as an end in itself, rather than as a means to build a "system."

With "systems," of course, our medieval sources abound, but the sources themselves are not systems; what animates the sources is a thought that has no intention of remaining imprisoned in its own creations. Thus in interpreting our sources, we should follow their lead and encounter them on the way, learning to see what they are seeing, or to direct our gaze to what they are gazing at, or to care for what they care for.

This does not mean that we should lose "scientific objectivity" to remain trapped in doctrinal factionalism. The original alternative to modern "empty" conceptual universalism is not tribal warfare. On the contrary, the question is one of *way*, of natural reason, of path leading from a superficial fragmented "objectifying" view of discourse to the recovery of discourse as inner life of the *permanent problems* addressed by our medieval sources. The goal is, in short, entering into the heart of our medieval sources, dwelling in them, being nourished by them, growing familiar with them and finally learning what it means to *be* what modern "compartmentalized" man would otherwise remain incapable of being.

## Notes

1 A parenthesis to the notorious "bashing" (*destructio*) of Plato by Aristotle: Jacob Klein once remarked that everyone knew that Aristotle lied. Understanding classical *rhetoric* is not the work of grammatical pedants, but of *poets* who read what is said in the light of the way "the what" is said, including the manner in which the said discloses its proper context. In short, the theatrical element of Plato's dialogues is not in the least alien from Aristotle himself, notwithstanding the Stagirite's use of the first person. Unless we concede that our classical authors are illuminating their "shared background" in speech, we are likely to end up attributing a context for them *ex machina*. In this case, the "attribution" is likely to severely inform our perception of what our authors are saying, if only by compelling us into conceiving "the what"

as uprooted from its triadic ground of system, hierarchy and proper telos. To return to Aristotle, it is not self-evident what the immediate context of his "bashing" was (one might cogently speculate that the Peripatetic was responding to vicious attacks on Plato, in a manner that could be, if not superficially reminiscent of Aristophanes's *Clouds*, then at least intimately related to the comedian's care to deflate vulgar hostility against Socrates by making a mockery of him).

2 Aquinas, *Sententia Libri Ethicorum* 1.11 (1098a23–25, Leonine edition).
3 For a list of more recent scholarship addressing the question of Aquinas's Platonism, see Doolan 2008, 29–30.
4 Fabro 2005.
5 Torrell has not been immune to the modern tendency. See Torrell 2008, "Saint Thomas et l'Histoire: État de la question et pistes de recherches" (originally published in *Revue thomiste*, 105 [2005]: 355–409): 131–75. Torrell fairly reproaches the neo-Thomism of the first half of the twentieth century for having sheltered Aquinas from "history." Yet, the error of neo-Thomists such as Aloîs Dempf, Jacques Maritain et Etienne Gilson did not consist in defending the atemporal character of Aquinas's discourse, but rather in effectively treating Aquinas's discourse as incapable of refuting its historicist detractors. Aquinas's new apologists would "defend" their hero from a historical context by robbing him of his *Platonic* one on the way to transplanting the medieval onto a Hegelian horizon (133).
6 These two extremes are found respectively in Vespignani 1887 and Henle 1970.

# 6 Introduction to the Problem of Context

Modern hermeneutics tends to aim at inscribing authors and texts by defining their "place" (cell, compartment, etc.) within a larger ever-evolving weblike context, or to "understand" literary sources by cutting them off from divine intelligence. Thereupon, understanding becomes essentially indistinguishable from domination serving the interests of self-empowerment. "Digesting" the sources takes primacy over being educated by them. The goal is to lower authors to the level of attention and expectations of readers, rather than for us readers to rise to the thought of our authors. "They" (the Other) are to feed us interesting means for the advancement of *our* cause(s). But what about the justice or injustice of our causes? Does encountering our literary Other not constitute a precious opportunity for us to *question* our own causes? Is it not to enter into *their* home, if only to better understand our own, without taking it for granted that *they* are unaware of a *common* home, or that they are incapable of helping us rise, of guiding us to consciousness of our common horizon as fundamentally intelligible? Now, the present study responds to such and similar questions by approaching its sources as interlocutors in a dialogue aimed at our rising to the overarching context of discourse as "world of pure intelligibility" or of "eternal ideas."

# 7 Medieval Platonism beyond Intellectual History

Writing in R. J. Henle's footsteps, in his *Aquinas on the Divine Ideas as Exemplar Causes*, Gregory T. Doolan proposed an intellectual history about various doctrines or "theories" that somehow converge in St. Thomas's own "theory" of ideas as "logically," though not "really" present in God in terms of "exemplar causes" of the empirical natures of things.[1] Unlike Duhem, Doolan presents and upholds Aquinas strictly as a full-fledged "philosopher," or rather he sets out to abstract a philosophical system from the *corpus thomisticum*, Thomas's collected works.[2] Yet, as an intellectual historian, Doolan replaces, if only unwittingly, philosophy with ideology, or a system of opinions aimed at solving philosophical problems. The "philosophy" he seeks categorically abstracted from "theology" (*ibid.*, xvii) is an empty shell conceived in the context of a purportedly universal and secular "history" that Aquinas would have readily perceived as but an imposter blinding us to the true nature of our twofold context as human beings, with the understanding that our "existential" context is known only in God (where existence is fully intelligible) and to some extent or another as the mind enters into God, as St. Bonaventure would put it.

But does Aquinas not read Aristotle as an intellectual historian? Did the Stagirite not offer us intellectual histories, if only in a sketchy form? The answer that should be obvious, but that is no longer obvious insofar as we consider the matter under the influence of modern *formae mentis*, is that Aristotle does not give us any intellectual history at all, but a review of *opinions* received from philosophy and probably via *non*-philosophers. And then Aristotle gathers those opinions to "populate" and organize a provisional stage for investigation of the truth underlying the opinions.[3] And in this, Aquinas, in the company of his medieval brethren, would agree fully, swearing that "the study of philosophy is not aimed at knowing what men have sensed, but in what way therein inheres the truth of things."[4] What really counts for St. Thomas is not who opined what, but the manner in which the truth of things inheres in opinions. Evidently, then, for the medieval writer, there are two planes to examine, or rather a twofold plane entailing a surface and a "latent" truth that uses the "grammatical" surface to invite us to discern truth itself, albeit not

DOI: 10.4324/9781003405689-8

as uninvolved in the constitution of the Letter of texts, but as involved in its organization *providentially*.

As long as we proceed as intellectual historians, we are doomed to fail to understand pre-modern writers who gathered opinions, as echoes of thought, to restitute dignity to those opinions in the context of a *dialogue* open to divine intellection.

Now, on Doolan's reading, Aquinas believed that Plato "posited his theory of ideas because of his concern to find certainty" given that the Greek "believed that all sensible things are in a state of flux" (45 anticipating 52–53). Aside from the hackneyed character of Doolan's latter point, his argument is based on a vulgarizing of his sources. As Aquinas saw well, Plato's Socrates appeals to eternal ideas to account for otherwise unprovable verities, not then for certainty as an end in itself, but to respond to skepticism *and* because he found no better way to speak of what things are in themselves.[5] Thus, red is what it is because of redness, which is a "form" that is evidently at once transcendent and immanent (to wit, all "reds" share "redness" and none could be itself without partaking in the common quality/form). Hardly a "theory" there, but merely an articulate expression of common sense. Thus the idea of "man" is that which all men share and in virtue of which each is himself. Or, again, all is one by partaking in unity; or, all *is* by partaking in *being* itself, which "is" in a pure or perfect manner, as opposed to any discrete or determinate being. Hence the thought of a being that is its own predicate, namely God. Again, hardly sufficient material for a "theory."

Unfortunately, Doolan misconstrues Plato's (and Aquinas's) ideas as "concepts" that are supposed to "exist" separately from "sensible thing" (*sensibilia*). In reality, neither Plato nor Aquinas presents ideas as existing concepts, or in a peculiarly *modern* fashion (naturally, existence entails motion and so imperfection).[6] Ideas are at once mirrors of things-themselves (what things really are) and that which the ideas mirror, namely their signification.[7] Otherwise put, ideas are at once *poetic* and *divine*, at once the best because proper way to speak of things *and* "things themselves," or things in a mind that is, as Aristotle would suggest, its own predicate: form of all forms, being of all beings, or "being in and of itself."[8] There is then no opposition between "universals" and "common natures." And so while Joseph Owens aptly disassociated Plato's ideas from their Thomistic replicas as *mere* universals (Doolan refers to Owens on p. 33), the Ideas are *at once* universal *and* common: at once poetic fictions and ontological foundations.[9] But Aquinas himself reaches this *Platonic* conclusion, if only by using a Platonic straw-man as steppingstone.[10]

Doolan chases after propositions, seemingly in the dark, in a visibly disoriented manner, trying to make sense of similarities and differences in a distinctively modern manner, or by reifying discourse out of a Platonic (natural-divine) context and into that of intellectual history, where thought itself is objectified, being conceived as one of its own determinations. Thereby, Aquinas's discourse ceases to be fundamentally coherent. But the medieval did not intend to be "coherent" in a modern sense, or by fitting all of his propositions into a "system of thought." There is no such system or "synthesis" for Aquinas, and not because, as Duhem would have it, the medieval *doctor* "failed" to attain to it, but because he never sought it to begin with.[11] Indeed, he would be firmly inimical to the thought of any such system; his own work reading, if anything, as expressive of a strenuous effort to oppose any tendency to reduce thought to any of its determinations. As is the case for both Plato and Aristotle, in whose footsteps walks Aquinas accepting no boundary for thought aside from thought's own divine perfection, even if this means that the project of "intellectual history" is blown asunder.

The "logic" of the modern "scientific" discipline of intellectual history, of history of *thought*, clashes against an unsurmountable mountain when confronted with medieval scholarship taken seriously and so understood as providing a fundamental *alternative* to our intellectual histories. Otherwise, the intellectual historian should reach Pierre Duhem's conclusion that Thomas Aquinas (representing legions of medieval Platonists "at heart" or *cordis*) was an eccentric master of idiosyncrasies, a synchretist resembling a blind child—certainly not a philosopher—who had integrated so many voices of the past as to merit being belittled as an eccentric master of idiosyncrasies.[12]

On Duhem's reading, the distinction between God and creatures represents a critical impasse in Thomism. While Duhem aptly recognizes that for Aquinas there is a categorical distinction between the perfection of creatures-as-such (finite beings) and that of God (being in and of itself), the French scholar concludes that Aquinas accounted for Christian uniqueness (*viz.* the Incarnation) by sacrificing a philosophical/rational cogency that would have otherwise required (as per Avicenna) that God have an essence, but not an existence (Duhem 1954: 510–11). So, considering Aquinas's work, Duhem concludes: "thenceforth, that distinction between essence and existence no longer played any role in the (Christian) theory of creation."[13] Why? Because existence was assumed to be present in God himself.

Whereas, in the case of finite beings, matter/content and idea/form can be perfected in tandem or harmonized, in God's case they coincide originally. In being-as-such (being-*qua*-being), existence is originally "resolved" in essence, as will is in intellect.[14] God *as such* does not exist as anything else does, but only in eternity. It is only vis-à-vis creatures and indeed *in* creatures that God "descends" from his heavens, if only to return to them.[15] For in creatures as *signs* of God inheres God's *reflection*, which by its own essence "returns" to God much as images in a mirror return to its source in which they are originally "at home" or perfect.

Duhem's objection to Aquinas is that the Dominican appeals to Aristotle to support a thesis that the Stagirite would seem to condemn, namely that of the separation of being and existence. For the Greek had sustained that "to be is none other than to be one" (οὐθὲν ἕτερον τὸ ἓν παρὰ τὸ ὄν, *Metaphysics*, Book 3.1). Now, Averroës (Ibn Rushd) read this to mean that, for all beings, to be is to exist, with the implication that there is no "essence" to which unity and being are added as "dispositions" (*dispositiones*): unity and existence are two ways of speaking of one and the same essence.[16] In arguing that to be (a) man is *eo ipso* to be *one* man, the Peripatetic would have suggested that there is no "essence" (form) of man aside from a determinate man (this "one" man). Yet, Aquinas (no less than Avicenna), distinguishes one existing man from man's essence, which thereby emerges as a "universal" (man in general). On the one hand, then, we have an "Aristotelian" appeal to the unity of being (to be is to be one) and on the other we have a "Platonic" distinction between being and existence given that the two can/must coincide in God alone.[17] This is the setup that Duhem objects to, if only by voicing bewilderment.

On a modern reading, Aquinas must have failed to speak coherently in the respect that he did not account for superficial contradictions in "clear and distinct" terms. On a pre-modern "poetic" reading, however, Aquinas's juggling of opinions invites the reader to open discourse to divine intellection.[18] If the medieval's "motivation" is not the one imputed to him by Duhem in accordance with modern expectations; if it is rather the opening of human speech (practical or "contextualized" reason) to divine speech (perfect intellection), then there may well be a way to make (rational) sense of Aquinas's "contradictions," or what Duhem sees as "numerous illogicalities" (*nombreux illogismes*).[19]

As suggested earlier, there is no necessary or fundamental contradiction between a poetic and a divine sense of terms. Given this principle of interpretation, Aquinas deserves praise for having maintained the poetic and the divine in positive (read, enlightening) tension lest either or both be obscured for us—as they are with Duhem, according to whom Aquinas finally "learned to prefer" "the logical perfection" of Aristotelians "to the poetic abundance of the discourses of Neo-Platonists" (*à la poétique abondance des discours néo-platoniciens*).[20]

Yet, in introducing abstract universals, far from departing from poetry, the scholastic is *de facto* confirming the ontological discrepancy between the human and the divine: only in God do essence and existence fully or properly coincide, whereas in man they coincide only *poetically*. Yet, where is God if not within the human, or at the bottom of my soul? In God (divine perfection of my own being), my being and my existence are truly one (my existence being "resolved" in my essence). But man is fallen, fallen into a world of ignorance, of compulsion, of madness, where the divinity of man is ubiquitously denied, obscured; or so it would be, were it not for a discourse that posits man's essence in God's own hands as supreme guarantors of man's existence. If "man" as "the human being as such" is not necessarily tied to any single man, then 1. he *must be* hidden eternally in God and 2. he *can be* manifest in a poetic "abstraction" mirroring the inherence of the man in God.[21]

Poetically speaking, the universal and the particular coincide, just as "dad" for the child is at once his own father and every other father; or "Caesar" for Roman citizens is at once Julius and every other emperor. It is our own inventive faculty that allows us to *abstract* images in which we begin discerning the infinite truth about finite beings, or the real being of beings in being-*qua*-being. So that the Platonist is right in asserting that the idea of man is transcendent with respect to any finite man, *and* the Aristotelian is right in teaching that there is no "man" outside of finite men, or no infinite being outside of finite ones. This is all to say that what is ordinarily perceived as finite is not ultimately finite, at all. But to "show" this to be the case we need poetic forms (as are originally "numbers"), which can remind us of the irreducibility of every being to its finitude, or to what we might call our "existential context," at the bottom of which every being is *being-itself* (much as for Socrates "manhood" or "the idea of man" is what any particular man really is).

## Notes

1 Doolan 2008, Ch. 3: "The Multiplicity of Divine Ideas" (83–122), passim. Doolan's reading of Aquinas, or rather of medieval Christian Platonism, is essentially *conceptualist* (Kantian-like), rather than Platonic. On the distinction at hand, see Katz 1998. On the reality of multiple relations in God, see *In Sent.*, Book 1, Dist. 26, Q. 2. Compare *ST*, 1, Q. 15, Art. 1, resp. and Art. 2, resp. where "many ideas are in the divine mind as its forms of intellection" (*plures ideae sunt in mente divina ut intellectae ab ipso*), as opposed to "visions" (*species*) affecting the understanding. To be sure, then, the *real* multiplicity of eternal ideas/forms in the divine mind is to be understood formally as a predicate of God, not the reverse, so that the multiplicity is in no way incompatible with unity (*non repugnat*). Yet, again, the divine mind is none other than the intellective act inseparable from its eternal forms, the multiplicity of which is the source, rather than the product, of the multiplicity of finite/empirical beings. On this latter point, see Boland 1996: 202–03.
2 This being said, Duhem himself sets out to abstract philosophy from theology (see *e.g.*, Duhem 2008, 568). What Duhem means by "philosophy," however does not coincide with what Doolan does. While, in the first case, philosophy tends to fall into the field of logical empiricism (positivism), in the latter it tends to shift *further* into the field of "trans-modern" (cf. foregoing reference) recreations of pre-modern discourse in the aftermath of the death of God announced by post-modernity.
3 As long as we proceed as intellectual historians, we are doomed to fail to understand pre-modern writers who gathered opinions, as echoes of thought, not to build "scientific systems," but to vindicate man's natural dignity in the context of a *dialogue* open to divine intellection.
4 "*Studium philosophiae non est ad hoc quod sciatur quid homines senserint, sed qualiter se habeat veritas rerum*" (*De caelo et mundo*, Book 1.22.8). Torrell 2008 ("Saint Thomas et l'Histoire," 154) tried and arguably failed to make Aquinas's statement serve the cause of intellectual history. Compare Aquinas's statement to Doolan 2008, 11: "For our purpose," writes Doolan, "we will take Henle's approach one step further. Since Thomas is at times aware of differences between the theories of Plato and the *platonici*, we will focus principally—not on what Thomas considers *Platonism* to be—but on what he considers to be the thought of Plato." It is uncertain to what extent if any Doolan succeeds in approaching thought as anything more or better than a complex system of opinions.
5 Doolan 2008: 24, remarks that Aquinas reads Plato's ideas as "explaining immobility (*immobilitas*)," rather than motion (*motus*). "Explaining" is not what Plato's ideas do, however—neither for Plato, nor for Aquinas; for, unlike modern

intellectual historians, neither Plato, nor Aquinas is bent upon constructing a "scientific" explanatory system. The aim is not akin to "building," but to *pure* or *intellectual contemplation* entailing vision of all things in the divine perfection of (their) being.

6 Consider for instance Aquinas, *Scriptum in primum librum Sententiarum*, dist. 36, Q. 2, Art. 2: "Whether there are Multiple Ideas" (*Utrum sint plures ideæ*), where the *existence* of creatures imitates the divine *essence* (in which all existence is gathered into perfection).

7 Upon this twofold nature of "ideas" rests much of the difficulty modern scholars have encountered in accounting for a classical and medieval understanding of "participation" without restricting participation to an abstract-concrete dynamics. See that is, "The Source of the Thomistic Notion (of Participation)," First Section ("Primary Sources") of Fabro 2005.

8 Doolan cites the most pertinent *Sententia libri Metaphysicae*, Lectio 10, n. 153.

9 *ST*, I, Q. 84, Art. 4. on the distinction between the idea-proper and its "imitation" (*similitudo*) within the finite being.

10 See pp. 218–21 of Owens 1959: 211–23.

11 Duhem 1954: 569.

12 See Duhem 1954: 569–70. Duhem wisely sought in Aquinas's *De ente et essentia* a point of access to the medieval's understanding of the relation between philosophical reason and biblical revelation. But Duhem's own formal aim is to reduce the *thought* of the *doctor angelicus* to a doctrinal summary, as opposed to encountering that thought in an irreducible dialogue . . . in the divine perfection of being itself (509). For an alternative recent fideistic reading of Aquinas's thought as a means to reduce philosophy (conceived doctrinally) to fuel for "personal experience in the life of faith," see DeSpain 2022 (cited from p. 23). For an attempt to read Maimonides (via Leo Strauss) as converting philosophy into an ideological support for liberalism, and in this sense as advocate of an "enlightened kalam" (where the Arabic *kalām* refers to a dialectical use of philosophy to support Islamic Law) see p. 67 of Millerman 2015: 51–69.

13 "Dès lors, cette distinction entre l'essence et l'existence n'a plus joué aucun rôle dans la théorie de la création" (*ibid.*).

14 More on this in pages to follow.

15 This lesson is discernible even in Aquinas's *De natura materi æ et dimensionibus interminatis opusculum*, Ch. 3. On Doolan's reading of Aquinas's divine unity as including multiplicity only "logically" beyond an existence conceived as metaphor of essence, it would seem that all we can know of God is logical patterns relative to, though also underlying the natural ones of created beings (2008: 117–22). The divine perfection of existence would then seem to pertain concretely to a divine unity beyond intelligibility, comparable to a Kantian *noumenon*.

16 Averroës, *Aristotelis Stagiritæ Metaphysicæ libri XII cum Averrois Cordubensis Commentaris*, Book 4, comm. 3. Cited in Duhem 1954: 523.

17 That Aristotle "returns" to a "separate" cause of finite beings (allowing us to speak of something's *transcendent* "essence") is well known by anyone even remotely familiar with the Stagirite's *Metaphysics*. Aquinas would of course be a solid supporter of the "return" in question. See Doolan 2008: 36 and 38. Doolan falls short of noting that just as Aristotle seeks the transcendent by turning to the immanent, so might Plato have sought the immanent by turning to the transcendent. As for Aquinas, suffice it to recall that his allegiance to both poles accords perfectly with his commitment to the Trinity.

18 This is a conclusion to which Rovighi 1965 opened the door, seeing Aquinas's appeal to "the unity of substantive form in man" (*l'unità della forma sostanziale nell'uomo*) as completing Aristotle's philosophical anthropology. But Rovighi falls

19 *Ibid.*, 567.

short of asking if, in developing the Stagirite's arguments, Aquinas did not perhaps somehow carry them all the way *back* to Plato (60–61).

20 Duhem 1954: 566. Duhem's Aquinas is *de facto* a proto-Positivist (and *explicitly* a precursor of early modern opponents of Scholasticism) representing a "simple and clear form" opposed to the "equivocations" of Platonists; and yet, Duhem's Aquinas fails to be the modern rationalist that his commitment to Christianity prevented him from becoming (566–67). On medieval scholars' "art of writing" beyond Duhem's all-too-modern dichotomy, see Strauss 1988. While Strauss concentrates on Arabic and Hebrew sources, there is no solid reason not to read Latin sources as seriously (and so as *poetically*) as Strauss read Maimonides. On this point, see Andreacchio 2021.

21 On Vico's reading, for the speakers of ancient Latin, "just as God is the crafter of nature, so is man the God of crafts" (*ut Deus sit naturae artifex, homo artificiorum Deus*): human art is the poetic, imperfect imitation of a divined perfect art. Vico 2005: 118.

# 8 Medieval Platonism

In his "Nature et grâce chez Thomas d'Aquin" ("Nature and Grace in Thomas Aquinas"), Jean-Pierre Torrell stressed the distinction between "the Greek tradition" not having been aware of our fallen condition and the Latin (pagan) tradition having been altogether skeptical of natural reason itself.[1] Now, bracketing expedient formal categorizations, it may be enlightening to admit the possibility that the Greek tradition addressed by Torrell was well aware of our fallen condition understood in emanational-Platonic terms. Plato himself would be the first to decry the condition of his Cave dwellers and the ineluctable discrepancy between Socrates's utopia and *any* polity on Earth. The question is not whether the Greeks were aware of our fallen condition, but whether they were aware of an original blessing independent of and *confirming* philosophers's dreams. Now, this question can hardly be settled by appeals to a traditional compartmentalization in the context of a Sacred History. For that History has been obscured in the supposed "broader" context of an *unqualified* History, beyond the medieval distinction between Sacred and Profane/Vulgar, as well as between Grace and Nature. Plato was not an idealist in the modern sense of the term, in the respect that he did not stand for the "historical" realization of "ideals," but for an onto-epistemic *return* to "things themselves" as Ideas in pure intelligibility. Nor was Plato by any stretch of the imagination a denier of divine providence within the human-political sphere. For he insisted that it is more profitable to be just, than to be unjust, or that justice is irreducible to power. This staple of Socratic argumentation entails the simple recognition that the corruption of the body does not carry with it by any necessity the corruption of the soul. In other words, "the Greek tradition" includes the staunch recognition of eternal life as heavenly ground for our everyday living.

Plato's image of man as a tree whose roots are planted in heaven should not be confused with the modern image of man whose "branches" reach out of the heavens. And while Socrates does not proclaim the incarnation of God as a man, he does point to the mysterious inherence of the divine in Socratic discourse.

Yet, what are we to say about Latin skepticism, the Roman refraining from metaphysical speculation? That refrain, too, is dubious, not to say evidently spurious. The Latin tradition did not reject the primacy of the contemplative over "the practical" (*praxis*), even as it placed a reasonable emphasis on the importance of the *ethical* as proper locus for metaphysical speculations. Those seeking to be wise should always remain pious and so honorable in the face of laws and republican institutions, if for no other reason, lest our institutions be left in the ravaging, impious hands of outright Philistines.

Let us grant, however, the figure of speech of Roman deniers of *any* access to divine intelligence and of Greek believers that man can turn himself into a God. The "middle ground" is represented by Christian awareness that our rational bond to the divine has been weakened by the Fall, but not altogether severed. The significant question here is not whether or not we have cognitive access to the divine, but how that access is to be understood. Is the distance between the political and the theological off limits to us? Radical skeptics would agree that it is. Torrell's Greeks would not.

It is not a matter of antiquarian curiosity to think through the problem at hand, but of returning to the problem of the inherence of grace in nature without taking either term for granted, or without fixing either term to any set of prejudices or expectations, such that could easily prevent us from appreciating the full scope and depth of either nature or grace.[2]

If the pre-Christian Platonist does not have the benefit of being confirmed in his ways by the Bible, must his "disadvantage" condemn him to an incapacity to be fully human, as Torrell suggests in line with an old traditional discourse? Is the Bible necessary for us to live fully virtuously, or is *any* pagan civil religion sufficient to allow fallen man to stand up on his own feet and walk upright and in the light of divine providence throughout the rest of his life, overcoming the perplexities and compulsions otherwise characteristic of fallen man? Assuming that grace is constitutive of nature, should the act of grace not be understood as extending beyond its Christian paradigm? Should we not rather seek it *through* that paradigm, as in a mirror? Should we not resist the temptation of dismissing the possibility that, though unacquainted with the Hebrew Bible, pagan philosophers were keenly aware of, or commonly turned-back-to the providential inherence of divine agency in human agency (beyond the vulgar view decried by Plato himself in his *Laws* of men as sheer marionettes of Gods)? And what if they were aware not merely of the inherence of the divine in the human, but also of man's incapacity to regain full access to divine unity?

Regardless of what the ancients "believed," however, it is their way of *living* problems that deserves scrutiny, if not the highest esteem. For their "answer" to our all-too-human condition was no totalistic settlement, but its nemesis *par excellence*: poetic reason as a life or "living word"[3]—as Aquinas would concur—mediating the human and the divine, as opposed to resolving the tension between the two poles, whether by collapsing either term into the other, or by establishing a higher synthesis of the two, not to speak of the postmodern alternative of dismissing both the human and the divine to "return" to a sub-human state of being.

## Notes

1 Torrell 2008: 127.
2 In Book 10.3 of his *Confessions*, St. Augustine guides the reader to discover human understanding as mediated by a hidden grace in the guise of divine care (*caritas*).
3 See further Augustine's *Confessions*, Book 13.2–3, where, through God's *sapientia/verbum*, all beings are given unity or being intellectively or by/in "illumination."

# 9 Medieval Platonic Hermeneutics

If all interpretation presupposes a context, medieval scholarship does not conceal its twofold *Platonic* one and the way it informs the work of the interpreter. The problem of interpretation is seated at the very heart of medieval Christian scholarship, which, far from being limited to defending mere beliefs against reason, rises to the challenge of seeking reason at the heart of the mystery of being in its absolute perfection. Such is the most intimate sense of St. Bonaventure's thirteenth century. "Journey of the Mind into God" (*itinerarium mentis in Deum*): the mind's return to God is none other than interpretation's return to the truth about its "outward" subject matter. For the human mind to return "into God" is for it to read the contents of everyday life experience back into perfect being as their original context. The interpreter is to "recollect" physical motion back into its principle or truth—the source of motion recognized as gift unfolding within its giver—much as those eating Eucharistic bread are to retrace the bread back to truth itself, the truth about the bread, or bread inherent in God himself; whence the invitation related in Luke 22:19, to "do this in remembrance of me" (*hoc facite in meam commemorationem*).[1] Platonically speaking, art (viz., the baker's own) sets the stage for our retracing physical nourishment to its divine source, gathering sensory motion back into its active principle, its principle of organization or intellection. Thus, too, does the interpreter gather the Letter or grammatical "surface of texts" (Torrell himself speaks of *la superficie des textes*, in this sense) back to its gravitational center as to the place where the Letter is set free—as Spirit, at once Word living in eternity.[2]

Medieval Platonic hermeneutics aims at overcoming the distance between the interpreter of a text and the Letter of the text, not by forsaking the sensory in the pursuit of nominal abstractions, but by raising the sensory back in a divine, original, sacred/secret context, namely thought undefiled by compulsions, mind itself unhampered by its own outward projections. To read Platonically would then be to perfect reading, to rise to the reading that God himself offers us, the very reading through which finite beings (ordered in their perfection, *in principio*) are offered to us so that we may rise through them to God.

Interpretation as journey of the mind into eternal being, or there where finite being is set free, is what medieval scholarship, from the classicist Boethius to Peter Lombard and Thomas Aquinas, can still teach us. Standing at the dawn of medieval scholarship, Boethius offers us a solid testimony of the philosophical-Platonic soul of Christian scholasticism, allowing us to discern a thread of Ariadne running from Saint Augustine's defense (*apologia*) of civilization (where we are reminded that we are not condemned to abide on any Tower of Babel, thereby mistaking power for truth, or collaboration for an end in itself) all the way to St. Thomas's monumental elevation of civilization—of both Reason and Authority, both Athens and Jerusalem—in a divine-like Cathedral, a fortified palace, veritable castle of conversations to which Dante would pay homage in the poetic evocations of *Inferno* 4, the Canto of the *nobile castello*: "castle of nobility."[3] Yet, Aquinas's thirteenth century Cathedral—whose most visible peaks are his *summae*—stands on the solid foundations laid out by Peter Lombard, twelfth century preeminent representative of the Christian Patristic heritage that Aquinas would embrace with a sacred mission: to vindicate the sacredness of civilization in the face of civilization's nominalist detractors, "Gentiles" who refused to admit any nobility that was not merely by convention.

In sum, to draw upon Boethius, Peter Lombard and Thomas Aquinas is to draw upon three pillars of Christian Platonism, or of Platonic interpretation in the light of Biblical revelation, a revelation that does not merely condone natural reason, but invites it rather to dare face the challenge of discovering all things in God as absolutely primary sense of being.[4] Thus understood, Revelation proclaims our common access to pure intelligibility, in terms of rational participation in divine being.

## Notes

1 To speak with St. Augustine, thinking is collecting memories into the mind as the mind gathers back into its own divine/creative perfection (*Confessions*, Book 10.11), which stands as a divine cradle of consciousness necessarily presupposed by the human mind (19).
2 Torrell 2008, "Saint Thomas et l'Histoire," 172.
3 See Andreacchio 2013a: 199–219. On the Platonism of medieval Aristotelian writers, see Leo Strauss's 1931 lecture on "Cohen and Maimonides" (republished in Green, ed. 2013: 173–222) where, "Strauss showed how he had begun to find a way to recover premodern rationalism. His point of departure was Hermann Cohen's suggestion that, contrary to popular understanding, the medieval Jewish philosopher Maimonides had been a Platonist rather than an Aristotelian. What made Maimonides a Platonist, Cohen argued, was the primacy he accorded to ethical and political questions, a concern ultimately rooted in the crucial question raised by Socrates, the founder of classical political philosophy: *How should I live?*" (Janssens 1966).
4 Leo Strauss would argue that the Scholasticism represented by Thomas Aquinas sought to defend the Bible before the tribunal of philosophy (see especially Strauss 1995). Strauss's argument falls short of highlighting a medieval effort to vindicate an original bond between human reason and divine intellection. Given that effort,

the scholastic defense of Revelation would amount to exposure of Revelation's providential import via-à-vis philosophy. Dante himself will carry Aquinas's work on beyond the Averroist reading of Revelation (Divine Law) as commanding us to philosophize. See Andreacchio 2021. On Averroës, see Butterworth's introduction to Averroës 2001.

# 10 The Problem of Creation

Participation of finite beings in being's perfection is disclosed by the question of mediation, or where the hiatus separating us from God ceases being a mere answer and converts into a question. No longer a matter of mere belief, the discrepancy between finitude and infinity emerges as a question to investigate, whereby infinity is no longer dreamed of as standing outside of finitude, but is sought as finitude's own perfection.

It is where God is divined as the infinite perfection of man that the question of purely-divine or perfect creation arises, beyond the limitations of human art. Yet the question of divine creation cannot be simply one among others, insofar as it remains constantly open to our investigations, constituting their primordial presupposition. In what sense does God "create?" What precisely does he create? What bearings do these questions have on our own lives, including our own speech and thus our own investigation? Does God's creative act inform our discussion about it? Over fifteen centuries ago, Boethius addressed such and similar questions, guiding future generations through a thoughtful exploration of an intimate alliance between human and divine art, including evidently that of speech.

As we heed Boethius we are called to confront the hiatus between God and Man as a primordial question filled with divine intellection itself. Yet, how can modern "historical" scholarship take that calling seriously? How can it transcend the contemporary dogma of a radical split between historical-scientific truth and religious ideas or beliefs, or even between "objective" Science and "subjective" Poetry? Bracketing our purported split phenomenologically, we ask if our reading of Boethius's addressing divine nature is affected by God's will beyond all reason, or by God's own Word providing our reason with access to its ground? Could that Word be at work in our own?

Let our own word remain consciously open, attentive to a divine mind mysteriously present within it. Thus speaks Boethius in his *Confession of Faith*:

The divine nature then, remaining from the eternal (i.e. from its eternal being) and within the eternal without any movement,[1] by a will known only within herself (i.e. within the divine nature), freely willed to establish order (reading "the world" as "order" *simpliciter*—TN)[2] and she made it so that it may be, since there was none at all, and neither did she produce it from her own substance, lest it be believed to be divine by (its own) nature, nor was it built from elsewhere, lest (it be believed that) something already existed that 1. helped her will by the existence of its own nature (as if there had been another divine nature—TN) and 2. be that which *is* without having been made from itself (i.e. as if there were a creature without creator—TN); for, by the *logos* it produced the heavens and created earth,[3] so as to establish worthy natures from heaven as celestial dwelling and so as to compose earthly things from earth.[4]

Boethius's passage contains a lesson cardinal to the challenge of thinking about causation, namely that volition is a function of intellection, whereby the emanation of all beings from their source—or the absolutely primordial mode of causality—is articulate, entailing not the reduction of alterity to unity (or the converse), but the original inherence of alterity in unity, which must thereby be, in principle, intelligible and thus *naturally good* insofar as the Good is that seat of knowledge that, as Aristotle signals in the opening verses of his *Metaphysics*, all men desire by nature.[5]

Now, modern thought, or the "grasping" of thought peculiar to the modern world, rejects the Good as a given end presupposed by (physical) motion. The rejection is based on a misconception identifying the Good with a *nominal* or "positive" guise of goodness, namely an absolute determination or *answer*, as opposed to an absolute indetermination or *question*.

Boethius's work testifies to medieval scholarship's capacity to orient modern readers to a divinity standing on the other side of our kaleidoscopic mirror of answers, as *first question*. God is First Question where all determinate beings are answers arising through an intellective act. Now, for our medieval Christian ancestors that act is the key to saving our answers from a state of utter alienation from the Good understood as "absolutely real being" (*ens realissimum*, to borrow Kant's expression): not merely as rational postulate, but as concrete providential agent in our daily lives and speech.[6] No authority, not even that of absolutely clear and distinct ideas, can prove to us the living presence of goodness in our lives. It is only in *dialogue* through trust in understanding—where *fides quaerens intellectum*—that we can discern the *existence* of the Good, not as domineering *deux ex machina*, but as the generous coincidence of language (and thus art) and nature that Saint Paul attests to in Galatian 2:20. Theologically speaking, God is present for us in a word (*verbum*) immutably produced by and returning to divine intellection, so that "the Son proceeds (from the Father) as the word of the Intellect" (*filius procedit ut verbum intellectus*).[7]

## Notes

1 If creation were understood as the conversion of nothing into something, then it would entail a mutation. Consider *ST*, I, Q. 45 ("Of the Way of the Emanation of Things from the First Principle"—*De modo emanationis rerum a primo principio*"), Art. 2 ("Whether God could Create Something"—*Utrum Deus possit aliquid creare*), obj. 2, where Aquinas presents an objection he will counter. The objection reads thus: "if to create is to make something from nothing, then to be created and arise as something. But all arising is a mutating. Therefore, creation is mutation. But every change is in some (determinate) subject, as is apparent from the definition of motion; for motion is the act of something existing in potentiality. Therefore, it is impossible for something to arise from God out of nothing" (*Si creare est aliquid ex nihilo facere, ergo creari est aliquid fieri. Sed omne fieri est mutari. Ergo creatio est mutatio. Sed omnis mutatio est in subjecto aliquo, ut patet per definitionem motus; nam motus est actus existentis in potentia. Ergo est impossibile aliquid a Deo ex nihilo fieri*). Aquinas responds that creation entails mutation only relatively to *our* intellection (*secundum intellectum tantum*, given a potentiality). The creative act as such involves no mutation or conversion of "nothing" into "something."
2 For the philosopher, "world" and "order" are interchangeable terms. Consider, however Lombard's words, where he writes: "Thus following (the biblical) tradition, let us inspect the order as well as the mode of the creation and formation of things. As recalled above, 'in the beginning God created heaven and earth'" (*Secundum hanc itaque traditionem, ordinem atque modum creationis formationisque rerum inspiciamus. Sicut supra memoratum est, 'in principio creavit Deus caelum, et terram*—op. cit., Book 2, Dist. 12.3). Is creation associated to order the way formation is associated to mode or way? Is formation the *way* that order is "created?" Is creation to be understood in terms of formation, if only *after* we inspect the order of words and way of speaking of tradition? Where "heaven and earth" are considered *together* (as opposed to being distinguished *philosophically*, as Boethius has done), ultimately is creation to be understood as the formation/establishment of order coinciding with the world itself ("heaven and earth")?
3 Writing as a philosopher, Boethius distinguishes the "production" of the heavens from the "creation" of earth (informed matter). In the former case, hidden forms are manifested; in the latter, physical forms are assembled into unities. This agrees with Aquinas's suggestions that formless matter is necessarily uncreated. Creation pertains to "informed-matter" which is thereby "matter" *shaped* in the light of an intelligible form in which form and matter are one. Such is "an idea in God."
4 "*Ergo divina ex aeterno natura et in aeternum sine aliqua mutabilitate perdurans sibi tantum conscia voluntate sponte mundum voluit fabricare eumque cum omnino non esset fecit ut esset, nec ex sua substantia protulit, ne divinus natura crederetur, neque aliunde molitus est, ne iam exstitisse aliquid quod eius voluntatem existentia propriae naturae iuvaret atque esset quod neque ab ipso factum esset et tamen esset; sed verbo produxit coelos, terram creavit, ita ut coelesti habitationi dignas coelo naturas efficeret, ac terrae terrena componeret*" (*Confessio fidei*, vv. 52–62 in Moreschini 2005).
5 Contemporary readers of Aquinas tend to mistakenly assume that Platonism's "emanation" is incompatible with Aristotle's lesson concerning the inherence of multiplicity in divine unity. A glaring example of the misconception in question is found in Brock 2006: 269–303.
6 For Aquinas, God's *existence*, as opposed to his *being*, is not an *a priori* of reason; it is, in other words, not absolutely necessary. It is through faith and thus trust that we can ascend (evidently *a posteriori*) to the thought, even certainty of God's existence. See Forgie 1995: 99–100.

7 *ST*, I, Q. 45 ("Creation"—*Creatio*), Art. 7 ("Whether in Creatures it be Necessary to Find the Vestige of the Trinity"—*Utrum in creaturis sit necesse inveniri vestigium Trinitatis*), resp. Contra Geiger, Doolan 2008, argues that for Aquinas God's Word is only "metaphorically" likened to divine ideas, as persons are to logical or strictly "philosophical" entities (117–22). But Doolan's Kantian-like reading of Aquinas is based on a misreading of his medieval source. See *e.g.*, Doolan's replacement of Aquinas's *qualified* sense of Word in the *De Veritate* (Q. 4, Art. 1), with an *un*qualified Word (119–20). Aquinas's (essentially Platonic) distinction between "God's ideas of things to be made" (*Dei ideae rerum faciendarum*) and "the word of the heart" (*verbum cordis*) is based directly on the distinction between "the externally expressed word" (*verbum exterius expressum*) and the Word as it is conceived by the intellect (*per intellectum concipitur*). Thus God's word is a metaphor of ideas only insofar as the word is conceived by the senses, as "voiced," rather than as hidden in the intellective act. In the latter case, the word *is* (really, not merely "logically") the ideas themselves. See Geiger 1974: 175–209. In his *Commentary on the Gospel of John*, Aquinas presents Aristotle explicitly as upholding divine ideas in God (*in deo rationes omnium rerum—Super Evangelium S. Joannis Lectura*, C. 1, Lect. 2); this is in full conformity with Aquinas's systematic "juggling" of Plato and Aristotle to point beyond their discrepancies. To wit: while Plato is presented as upholding eternal forms and Aristotle as placing them in God, Aquinas sets out to restore the *Platonic* distinction between 1. the *original* forms of things and 2. forms that carry with them "the world" (*mundus*)—i.e., the created order of things "out of" God—lest *our* world be misconstrued as "coeternal" (*coaeternus*) with divine ideas. In short, Aquinas is restoring Aristotle "in Plato." On the use of "Plato" and "Aristotle" as literal signposts for argumentation—where the former philosopher represents the view that the universe is in a state of temporally infinite flux, while the Peripatetic represents the view that the universe is overall simply eternal—see Maimonides, *Guide*, 2.13. ii-iii. In Ch. 15, Maimonides explicitly denies that Aristotle *believed* his opinions to be conclusive. Yet, Maimonides's professed aim is not to establish his own opinion as truth beyond the opinions attributed to Plato and Aristotle, but to show that the (biblical) view that the universe is created altogether by God (and so the doctrine of *creatio ex nihilo*) is *superior* in worth to its categorical denial as voiced *Aristotelians* who are logically forced to see the universe *a posteriori*, or extrinsically, shutting themselves to thought about the universe in God's mind, or on the plane of pure intelligibility. (It is worthwhile noting that Maimonides opens his discussion on the problem of creation from nothing with a warning about the key problem of "time," which is not to be misconstrued as existing in and of itself, given that it is merely the attribute of an attribute, or a function of the motion of things.) On Aquinas's familiarity with Maimonides's work, see Sermoneta 1969. See further Burrell 1988.

# 11 Creation from Nothing?

While in a derivative or non-primordial sense, generation and creation are two distinct acts, in a primary sense they coincide. Thus does Aquinas write:

> For in generation, what is generated receives the nature of the generator, which is of perfection; yet in creation the creator does not mutate, though the created does not receive the nature of the creating agent. It is thus said that the Son is at once created and generated, since from creation is received the immutability of the father and from generation the unity of nature in both Father and Son.[1]

In creating, God remains immobile or lacking mutation insofar as what he alters is other than himself;[2] in generating, God is immanent in the generated, whence "the unity of nature between Father and Son." In an ordinary, "fallen" context, generation entails mutation, while creation entails separation. Transcendence and immanence are then mutually incompatible. Yet, where creation is through generation, immanence and transcendence coincide: the source is at once entirely or immediately present in the sourced (generation entailing self-contained self-giving), while the "product of art" or the "created being" is none other than the source's own living presence. If the Father were not entirely present in the Son, then the Son would represent a mutation with respect to the Father. But how can the Father be entirely Son without being reduced to the Son? The answer is given by "creation," albeit one whereby the "matter" is none other than the creator. Where the creator is the matter itself, the created being is of the same nature as the creator.[3] The Father empties himself entirely in the Son who is at once generated and created, so that creation is *immediate emanation*.[4]

Whereas in a derivative or "fallen" sense creation and generation, as art and nature, are distinct, in an absolute, primordial sense, the creative act is *ex nihilo*, which is to say that there is "nothing" outside of the creator constituting the source of the product of art, which will be *eo ipso* alive. Nature itself is alive insofar as its primordial or divine source is entirely present in it. But then nature is not a mere body and certainly not a machine, insofar as it *incarnates*

DOI: 10.4324/9781003405689-12

its absolute source. Yet, again, there is a "pivot" accounting for the discrepancy between nature in its original sense and nature in its "fallen" sense. That pivot is the Son, second person of the Trinity. Through the Son, nature is restored to its immaculate conception, even as the Son enters into our fallen world through nature itself, or rather *her*self, showing that nature is originally immaculate. How does the Son show that nature is immaculate? By testifying to the *full* presence of the Father in the Son. That presence could never be established unless nature were devoid of obstacles, interferences rendering the generative act mediated and thus involving mutation. The immediacy of divine generation, as opposed to merely-physical generation, entails the purity of nature, which is to say, of the "womb" of generation. Yet, nature's purity does not erase the transcendent dimension of nature's source. Nature is "created" insofar as it remains *other* with respect to its mysterious source, even as that source remains providentially at work in nature—as an artist working from within his creation.

It is by way of showing that nature is neither simply divine, nor simply other than the divine, that the divine is revealed as Son, Savior of all those who renounce all mechanistic conceptions of nature—indeed of both creation and generation—to espouse a conception of nature as *meaningful life*, or generation that is "created" from within, or *ex nihilo*, which is to say, through immediate emanation and so without relying on any "external matter"—as if God were a deist "ideal" or "value" intervening *ex machina* to "explain" the *factum brutum* of nature as machine.[5]

Aside from the second person of the Trinity, things are merely created by God, as opposed to being also generated; not because generation is something fundamentally other than creation, but because *for us* creation is an "extrinsic" act, whereby the creator stands outside of his creation. Hence Aquinas's emphasis on distinguishing creation *ex nihilo* from divine filiation, which involves, as seen, both creation and generation, even as *for us* generation (*generatio*) and creation (*creatio*) never coincide:

> Now, just as a created artisan makes something out of matter, so does God make (beings) out of nothing . . . not as if this nothing yielded the substance of the thing, but because by him the whole substance of a thing is produced, without anything else presupposed. Thus if the Son proceeded from the Father as something existing out of nothing, then the Son would be to the Father as an artifact is to the artisan, where evidently the designation of "filiation" would not apply, unless by some kind of similitude. Hence, we conclude that, if the Son of God proceeded from the Father as if he existed from nothing, then he would not be truly and properly a Son. . . . The Son of God is therefore not from nothing, nor is he made, but strictly generated. And if those who are made from nothing by God are called sons of God, this would be metaphorically, according to some assimilation to

he who is the true son. Hence is he called "uniquely generated," inasmuch as he is the only true and natural Son of God.[6]

Aquinas's defense of the proposition that God "creates from nothing" responds, at least at first glance, to classical philosophers' affirmation that "nothing is produced from nothing" (*ex nihilo nihil fieri*), where one might deduce (*ergo*) that "God cannot make or create anything out of nothing" (*Deus non potest aliquid ex nihilo facere, vel creare*). Yet, contrary to what modern readers might expect, Aquinas's defense relies upon philosophers, rather than upon any theological appeal to divine volition. What "creation from nothing" ultimately means is what Platonic philosophers invoke as *ultimate derivation from God*:[7] all things are entirely retraceable to God as to their source, *whether or not* they pass by a divine will, for this passing remains, here, an open, unaddressed question. What is more, evidently, not everything is "created" by God in a narrow sense of the term "create," for we have what is *generated* (produced directly) by God as the Word in which and through which the divine Intellect or Volition/Freedom manifests itself. Pertinent arguments are found in *ST*, I, Q. 45 ("Of the Mode of Emanation of Things from the First Principle"), Art. 1, where "creation" is *direct emanation*, as "act" from God, rather than autonomous establishment through any volitional act, or free will: "We must consider, not only the emanation of some particular being from some particular agent, but also the emanation of all beings from a universal cause, which is God, and this emanation we designate by the name of creation" (*non solum oportet considerare emanationem alicuius entis particularis ab aliquo particulari agente, sed etiam emanationem totius entis a causa universali, quae est Deus, et hanc quidem emanationem designamus nominee creationis*).

Aquinas goes on qualifying the reason why "from nothing" is said of divine creation. The reason is that, as in human generation, divine generation does not presuppose a third something (*aliquod ens*), mediating the source and the sourced. The generation of son from father does not presuppose anyone else (neither another father, nor another son). "But that which proceeds from a particular emanation is not presupposed by the emanation; as where, if a man is generated, he was not previously a man, but a man arises out of a non-man" (*Quod autem procedit secundum emanationem particularem, non praesupponitur emanation; sicut si generatur homo, non fuit prius homo, sed homo fit ex non homine*). The man as man, or as a whole, is new and springs *directly* from the father.

Of course, in the case of the *physical* father we can easily object that "other factors" are involved in generation, which is "in time" (for Jesus exists outside of Joseph). However, in the case of *divine* generation, which pertains to the totality of beings, or even to the totality of every being, temporal distance is not a pertinent factor. When it comes to the generation or production of the totality of beings (and thus of the cause of all things conceived together, as a "universe"), there is no third, independent party at play; none mediating God and the Order/World he produce. Hence Aquinas's conclusion:

> Therefore, just as the generation of man proceeds from a determined-being that is not (*ex non ente*), which is a non-man, so creation, which is the emanation of all being (*totius esse*), is from a being that is not (*non ente*), which is 'nothing' (*sicut igitur generatio hominis est ex non ente, quod est non homo, ita creatio, quae est emanatio totius esse, est ex non ente, quod est nihil*).[8]

## Notes

1 "*In generatione enim, quod generator accipit naturam generantis, quod perfectionis est; in creatione vero creans non mutator, sed creatum non recipit naturam creantis. Dicitur ergo filius simul creatus et genitus, ut ex creatione accipiatur immutabilitas patris, et ex generatione unitas naturae in patre et filio*"—*ST*, I, Q. 41 ("On Persons in Comparison with Nominal Acts"—*De Personis in comparatione ad actus notionales*), Art. 3, resp. 4; restated in *Summa Contra Gentiles*, Book 4, Chapter 8.
2 Creation does not entail any mutation (*creatio non est mutatio*), whether of non-being into being, or of being into non-being.
3 "The Son is generated of the essence of the Father, inasmuch as the essence of the Father communicated to the Son through generation subsists in him" (*filius est genitus de essentia patris; inquantum essentia patris, filio per generationem communicata, in eo subsistit*—*ST*, I, Q. 41, Art. 3, ad. 2).
4 Immediate emanation properly understood entails not the totalistic assimilation of freedom to necessity (relying on conventional readings of Platonism, Torrell 2008 falls short of discerning this much), but the immediacy of providential agency, which, as medieval scholasticism argues at length, does not preclude but make good use of secondary causes, with the understanding that the human being is irreducible to a secondary cause, as the significantly-*Platonist* Pico della Mirandola would not tire to remind us. See Andreacchio, Winter 2021. For in the unique case of man/Adam, the secondary cause is at once primary insofar as our reason is one with divine intellection. In human mediation (virtue or prudence), divine providence gives itself entirely so that it may "see" through "created" eyes (through another's eyes, or dialogically) distinctions that it would otherwise remain blind to, as law per se must be. In this fundamental intuition we find an extreme vindication of the Chalcedonian principle that "the natural element and the divine element are united without confusion but also without separation in the unique reality of the being recipient of grace" (*l'élement naturel et l'élement divin sont unis sans confusion mais aussi sans séparation dans l'unique réalité vivante de l'être gracié*"—Torrell, *NG* (99–129), 114. Torrell is prompt to add that "we shouldn't push too far the parallel with the ontological constitution of Christ, for contrary to the divinity in him, grace in us can be lost" (*il ne faudrait pas pousser trop loin le parallèle avec la constitution ontologique du Christ, car contrairement à la divinté chez lui, la grâce chez nous peut se perdre*). As Torrell might well agree (*cf.* 126), what remains to be investigated is the nature of the categorical distinction, not merely between Christ and *any* man in the state of corruption, but also and most importantly between the Christ and less paradigmatic heroes.
5 Naturally, creation *ex nihilo* is opposed to any creation *ex machina*.

6  "*Sicut autem artifex creatus facit aliquid ex materia, ita Deus facit ex nihilo ... non quod nihilum cedat in substantiam rei, sed quia ab ipso tota substantia rei producitur, nullo alio praesupposito. Si ergo filius procederet a patre ut de nihilo existens, hoc modo se haberet ad patrem ut artificiatum ad artificem, quod manifestum est nomen filiationis proprie habere non posse, sed solum secundum aliquam similitudinem. Unde relinquitur quod, si filius Dei procederet a patre quasi existens ex nihilo, non esset vere et proprie filius. . .. Filius igitur Dei verus non est ex nihilo, nec factus, sed tantum genitus. Si qui autem ex nihilo a Deo facti filii Dei dicantur, hoc erit metaphorice, secundum aliquam assimilationem ad eum qui vere filius est. Unde, inquantum solus est verus et naturalis Dei filius, dicitur unigenitus*"—*ST*, I, Q. 41 ("On Persons in Comparison with Notional Acts"—*De personis in comparatione ad actus notionales*), Art. 3 ("Whether Notional Acts Proceed from Something"— *Utrum actus notionales sint de aliquo*), resp.
7  See Aquinas's *De Aeternitate Mundi*, cited in Soars 2020: 950–66; 952–53.
8  Given the immediacy of the primal act of causation, Aquinas, no less than Maimonides, could speak of God's agency independently of any created universe, or even under the assumption that the universe is eternal; with the understanding that our ascent to God is not ultimately affected by our opinion about the universe being created or not—even though our opinion could have dire *practical* or ethical-political consequences (Maimonides, *Guide*, 2.25). See Seeskin 2012. Yet, Maimonides's argument should not be construed to suggest that the universe can be adequately understood aside from divine providence. On Seeskin's reading, Maimonides is open to a (future) "physics" capable of accounting for our universe (thereby providing a reasoned explanation for its being the way it appears to us) independently of any reference to God, whereby "physics" could disclose the *truth* about Scripture/Torah (192–93 and 197–98). This conclusion presupposes a peculiarly *modern* ("scientific") conception of physics, as opposed to a classical (incl. medieval) *poetic* conception on account of which there can be *reasonable* or *likely* accounts of the universe, but not *the* true and final one, given that the primal mode of causation of things transcends the strictures of any formal logic, being rather "defined" by the *virtus* of divine intellection itself. And this we can easily intuit when considering the way classical painters produce their masterpieces. So, in accepting the "logical possibility" that the universe is eternal, Maimonides, no less than Aquinas (*ibid*. 199) would not be open to any atheistic account of our world, but to a "beatific vision" (to speak most notably with our *doctor angelicus*) whereby the world emerges mysteriously "in God" as God's own eternal *content*; so that—to cite Seeskin, 194—the universe would "in some deeply esoteric sense *be* God." On Maimonides's upholding the definite primacy of both reason and revelation over what we would calls "scientific truth," see pp. 239–41 of Gluck 1998. In citing Maimonides's *Guide* 2.24, Green himself (in Green ed. 2003, 428) presents Maimonides as suggesting that perhaps *one day* physicists will attain to a knowledge of the heavens (thus of cosmic motion) allowing us to settle once and for all the question of the origins or permanence of the universe. Yet, Maimonides's argument effectively, if only subtly, steers the reader away from any possible "perfect science" of the heavens, unless by that expression we are referring to a mystical, intimate, living divine communication. While Maimonides does leave open the possibility of a perfect physics, *de facto* he discounts it entirely on account of man's limited faculties, by which he could hardly be referring to our "tools," but to our mortality, or our need to relate the heavens to the earthly, which is to say to our ethical-political context, in order to make sense of the heavens. Indeed, in citing the *Guide* 2.25 where Maimonides claims he could read Genesis 1 "figuratively" to imply the eternity of the world, Green tacitly invites the thought of a parallel between figurative readings of the Bible and the way we *as-men* (thus always) are limited to read the heavens.

# 12 Divine Creation as Key to Freedom

The generation of a determined-being (*entem*) presupposes the act of generation of *all* being, or being *as a totality*, or being "in general." The earthly father's generation presupposes and is supported by a primordial sense of generation. Here is the crux of the matter: emanation or generation is not adequately understood as "physical" (or particular), but via a *universal* in which we begin discerning the absolute sense of generation, or what generation is in itself, namely a gift in which the giver projects itself entirely, as opposed to a process separating the giver from the gift.[1] Hence the doctrine of the Trinity, in which the Giver and the Gift are one in the Giving. Aquinas's appeal to the Bible or the biblical tradition (the two are *de facto* equivalent, for him) is an appeal to the *word* in which the Gift and the Giver are one—as "particular" (Son) and "universal" (Father), or as Man (physical father) and God (divine father). In the *act* that is none other than "divine poetry" or creation-as-*logos*, the source and its sourced coincide. *This* is the crux of the doctrine of "creation from nothing." That doctrine is not about a will separating creator from creature, but about a mysterious *living word* through which and in which creator and creature coincide. Hence Boethius's reading of the divine nature's "free will" in terms of *verbum*. What is "freedom" *for us* is immutable necessity *for God*. For his agency exudes from his nature and returns within it (*her*) without any alteration/mutation, or motion. Hence Boethius's *sine aliqua mutabilitate*: "without any mutation or motion," "utterly unmoved" (as per Aristotle) and in this sense "freely" (whence Boethius's *sponte*). Properly understood, the divine will entails the immediacy of the divine act, inviting at once a distinction between creator and creature *and* open access between the two, which is to say *divine providence*, on the one hand, and *human freedom* (human providence), on the other. In the absence of the immediacy of the divine act, human freedom would have no foundation, since man would have no conscious access to the content of divine nature. Man could not participate in or respond meaningfully to the divine. Hence Aquinas's defense of human freedom as essentially bound to the divine. In the words of Peter Lombard:

> True free choice is the faculty of reason and will, by which the good is chosen with the assistance of grace, or evil in the absence of the same.

DOI: 10.4324/9781003405689-13

And it is said to be free, with respect to the will, which can be bent indeterminately (*ad utrumlibet*).[2] But choice, with respect to reason, is that faculty or power of he who also has the ability to discern between good and evil, and indeed sometimes having discernment between good and evil, he chooses what is evil, but sometimes what is good. Yet, he does not choose what is good unless grace is adjoint, but he chooses evil by itself. There is therefore in the rational soul a natural will that naturally wants the good, even if weakly and feebly unless grace helps; (and that grace) intervening helps (the will) and raises it to want the good effectively (i.e. carrying out good decision—TN). But (where the object of choice is—TN) on its own (i.e., devoid of grace—TN), it is possible to will evil effectively (thereby *doing* evil—TN). That power of the rational soul by which (the soul) can will good or evil, discerning between the two, is named free choice, which brutish animals do not have, since they lack reason, although they have sense and sensual appetite.[3]

## Notes

1 The process or "evolution" alienated from the living agency of divine intelligence must be mechanical.
2 On the relative independence of what is *ad utrumlibet* from divine providence, see Posti 2020 (esp. pp. 50, 70–71, 92 and 154). Divine providence, but not its human counterpart, is perfectly conceivable in the absence of the element of chance in the constitution of the physical universe. On the *coincidentia* of divine providence and human providence in "the intellect," see further Maimonides, *Guide*, 3.17. On Maimonides's doctrine of providence in relation to ancient and Islamic sources, see Strauss 2004: 537–49.
3 "*Liberum verum arbitrium est facultas rationis et voluntatis, qua bonum eligitur gratia assistente, vel malum eadem desistente. Et dicitur liberum, quantum ad voluntatem, quae ad utrumlibet flecti potest. Arbitrium vero, quantum ad rationem, eius est facultas vel potentia illa, cuius etiam est discernere inter bonum et malum, et aliquando quidem discretionem habens boni et mali, quod malum est eligit, aliquando vero quod bonum est. Sed quod bonum est nisi gratia adjunta non eligit, malum vero per se eligit. Est enim in anima rationali voluntas naturalis, qua naturaliter vult bonum, licet tenuiter et exiliter, nisi gratia juvet; quae adveniens juvat eam, et erigit ut efficaciter velit bonum. Per se autem potest velle malum efficaciter. Illa ergo rationalis animae potentia, qua bonum vel malum potest velle, utrumque discernens, liberum arbitrium nuncupatur, quod bruta animalia non habent, quia ratione carent; habent tamen sensum et appetitum sensualitatis*"; Lombard 1841. See further Aquinas, *In Sent.*, Dist. 24.1, Proem.

# 13 What is Freedom?

Peter Lombard presents choice as based on discernment, which depends, in turn, upon the grace of divine intellection in which, as Aquinas reminds us, freedom and necessity coincide. Thus in his *De Veritate* ("Of Truth"), Q. 24 (*De libero arbitrio*—"Of Free Choice"), Art. 1 ("Whether in Man There Be Free Choice"—*Utrum in homine sit liberum arbitrium*), sc. 2, Aquinas shows that our own freedom is situated between God's absolute freedom—which involves creation of or out of itself—and natural necessity, which in and of itself has no place for freedom. Whereas our own freedom is exercised through the effort to order what is outside of our faculty/freedom, God's freedom effortlessly orders what is within its own scope/agency (in this sense God *can* all that he *wants*; for what he wants is *rationally* within his reach, which is to say that God does not irrationally want what he cannot achieve).[1]

To return to Lombard's articulation of the problem of free choice/arbitration, it is evident that human freedom requires the intervention of grace, without which the object of choice is likely to be evil. Why? And why is the good unaccompanied by grace insufficient to keep us on the path of righteousness? If our *seeing* what is good is not enough for us to *do* what is good, then something more than an outer good is needed to attract us to do good. That "supplement" is grace (*gratia*)—by definition a "free gift"—which can be nothing other than the intellective act manifest in the divine *verbum*, the Word in which eternal being presents itself before us, thereby enabling us to carry our freedom to fruition. Outside of the context of the Word as *logical articulation* of God among men—or more concisely, as *theological-political dialogue*—we rely on the mere *appearance* of the good, or on the good as Other with respect to our capacity to partake in divine intellection. As a result, our capacity remains virtually hapless in the face of "temptation." We are then dreadfully gullible, all too easily deceived by appearances. When, on the other hand, what we see is supported by grace and so restored in the context of the Word among men, then we *naturally* choose what is good and freely carry out our choices. Thereupon we manifest our "rational nature, which acts from a presupposed matter, though not from necessity, but from freedom of choice" (*nature rationalis natura, quae agit ex praesupposita materia, et non ex necessitate, sed ex arbitrii libertate*). For then we are no longer compelled as "brutish animals" (Lombard's *bruta animalia*) to follow sensual impulses. Instead, we see the good as something that does not merely *feel* good (even as it is not a merely nominal, painful imposition upon our senses), because it *is* good in the respect that in it freedom and necessity, as art and nature, are divinely conjoined. But this conjoining is none other than the providential intellective agency of eternal being that, in all particular circumstances of life, shows us the narrow path leading back to it.

It is in following a good that is at once pleasant and just ("legal") that man is free, exercising his proper *political* function, which necessarily involves facing both determinate good and evil, and thus both the lawful and the lawless (keeping in mind St. Paul's distinction between Jews and Greco-Romans),[2] in the light of a divine, indeterminate good—our First Question. Man will not "solve" the problem of evil, thereby establishing the good as an absolute *determination*, but *order* empirical determinations into a political order—both legal and moral—reflecting the order of eternal being. Not being a mere angel, man does not attend only to first causes, being called *by nature* to relate "inferior things" to them, thereby establishing a world or order (*mundus*) characterized by the primacy of what is more intelligible over what is less intelligible, as well as of higher intelligence over lower intelligence.[3] For,

> it must be that the ultimate happiness of man that is possible to have in this life consists in the consideration of first causes, for the little that can be known of them is more lovable and more noble that all of the things that can be learned of inferior things.[4]

As angels, we are capable of turning toward God, even though, unlike heavenly angels, we turn to God in the act of attending to evil.[5] For man alone lives "politically," thus responding to and partaking in divine grace through a heroic effort involving, evidently, not contemplation alone, but also animal sentiment. Nor are we told, in our primal created condition, to turn to God, for there is no "natural law" that determines our choice, as is deducible from Lombard's own account of *liberum arbitrium*, where he writes:

> For (soon after Creation) all had free choice, which is the free power and ability of the rational will. For they could choose anything by the will, and judge by reason, that is, discern, which is what free choice amounts to, and they were created not wanting to be turned away from or turned toward (their creator), but capable of wanting this or that; and after Creation, by spontaneous will some chose evil, others good; and so God distinguishes light from darkness, as Scripture says, that is, good angels from bad; and he called light day, but night darkness (*Genesis* 1), because he illuminated the good angels by his grace, but blinded the evil ones.[6]

"Spontaneous will" (*spontanea voluntas*) is only partially, if not accidentally what causes "some" to choose evil, while others good. For, in order to guide us well our reason and will require, not only an apparent or formal good, but also the grace of intellect, which shines in our "fallen world" but imperfectly.[7] For unlike its divine counterpart, our world is not ruled by strict necessity, so that God cannot intervene as he does in his heavens. In *our* world, divine grace rules by illuminating *some* minds more than others, and thus by calling some to guide and govern others, which is to say to exercise *human* providence, or free choice illuminated by divine grace. For the divine will cannot function where divine intellection does not shine—a lesson we can glean from Aquinas's "Of the Will of God," where we read:

> I answer by saying that will is (*voluntate esse*) in God, just as intellect is in him; for will follows from (*consequitur*) intellect ... will must be in God, since intellect is in him; and just as intellect is his being, so is his being his volition (*velle* ...) for divine will is necessarily related to its goodness, which is its proper object. Hence God wills his goodness out of necessity ... and God wills things other than himself insofar as they are ordered unto his goodness as end ... God wants all good things that arise, to arise. If, therefore, his will imposed necessity on the things willed, it would follow that all good things come of necessity; and thus perishes free choice and counsel and all such things.[8]

Where volition is a function of intellection, the divide between Aquinas and Platonism vanishes in principle. For then, divine creation entails an emanation in which artistic freedom and natural necessity are reconciled without being synthesized.[9] Yet, the doctrine of "creation from nothing" is usually construed as being opposed to "Neoplatonic" teachings presenting world/order as stemming "genetically" from the divine, most notably via an "emanation."

## Notes

1. On modern reason wanting irrationally what it cannot achieve (because it does not properly belong to it), see Jolivet 1935: 71. Modern reason/science seeks to appropriate for itself (viz., in "technological empowerment") an intellective act that, for our medieval authors, is presupposed by and never resolved in reason, be this human or post-human. The problem of the proper or original relation between reason and intellect is one that "modern speculation has mostly confused" (*que la speculation moderne a surtout émbrouillé—ibid.*, 182).
2. Evidently the lawless does not necessarily imply evil, but an unchecked or inadequately checked propensity for erring.
3. On the superiority of man over angel, see Aquinas, *In Sent.*, Book 3, Dist. 14, Art. 3, q. 2, obj.: "Being a man, Christ teaches angels. Therefore, he has greater knowledge than them" (*ipse Christus secundum quod homo, docet Angelos. Ergo majorem scientiam habet quam illi*).

What is Freedom?   61

4  Aquinas, *Super librum De causis expositio*, Proem: "*Opertet . . . quod ultima felicitas hominis quae in hac vita haberi potest, consistat in consideratione primarum causarum, quia illud modicum quod de eis sciri potest, est magis amabile et nobilius omnibus his quae de rebus inferioribus cognosci possunt.*"
5  Evidently, fallen angels attend to evil without turning to God. In this respect, man is in some way luciferin. On "Lucifer" (bearer of light) as classical poet, see Andreacchio 2012: 55–82.
6  "*Habebant enim [post creationem mox] omnes liberum arbitrium, quod est libera potestas et habilitas voluntatis rationalis. Poterant enim voluntate eligere quodlibet, et ratione judicare, id est discernere; in quibus constat liberum arbitrium, nec creati sunt volentes averti vel converti [ad creatorem suum], sed habiles ad volendum hoc vel illud; et post creationem spontanea voluntate alii elegerunt malum, alii bonum; et ita discernit Deus lucem a tenebris, sicut dicit Scriptura, id est, bonos angelos a malis; et lucem appellavit diem, noctem vero tenebras, Gen. 1, quia bonos angelos gratia sua illuminavit, malos vero excaecavit*"—Lombard, *op. cit.*, Book 2: "Of the Creation and Formation of Physical and Spiritual Things and of Many Other Pertinent Subjects" (*De rerum corporalium et spiritualium creatione et formatione aliisque pluribus eo pertinentibus*), Distinctio 5.2.
7  John 1:5 and 3:19.
8  "*Respondeo dicendum in Deo voluntate esse, sicut et in eo est intellectus; voluntas enim intellectum consequitur . . . oportet in Deo esse voluntatem, cum sit in eo intellectus; et sicut intelligere est suum esse, ita suum esse est suum velle . . . voluntas enim divina necessariam habitudinem habet ad bonitatem suam, quæ est proprium ejus objectum. Unde bonitatem suam Deus ex necessitate vult . . . alia autem a se Deus vult, in quantum ordinantur ad suam bonitatem ut in finem . . . omia bona quæ fiunt, Deus vult fieri. Si igitur eius voluntas imponat rebus volitis necessitatem, sequitur quod omnia bona ex necessitate eveniunt; et sic perit liberum arbitrium, et consilium, et omnia hujusmodi*"—*ST*, I, Q. 19 (*De Dei voluntate*—"On God's Will"), Art. 1 (*Utrum in Deo sit voluntas*—"Whether Will is in God"), resp.; Art. 3 (*Utrum quidquid Deus vult, ex necessitate velit*—"Whether whatever God wills, he wills by necessity"), resp.
9  Brock 2006: 302.

# 14 Emanationism vs. Voluntarism

Daniel Soars recently questioned this modern construal, reminding us that the doctrine of *creatio ex nihilo* originally and traditionally meant to refute, not the divine source of the world, but the retracing of the world to any source other than the divine.[1] What Boethius's passage cited earlier from his *De Fide Catholica* shows is that the divine source of the world (or of *mundus* as order/*ordo*) is to be understood as *intelligible*, which is to say that "creation" (not Boethius's term, in the passage under consideration) is to be understood in terms of *logos/verbum*, the living Word of God. Boethius objects to the conflation of world and divinity insofar as a teaching conflating the two would present the world as unintelligible. For the world (indeed, the very notion of order) is intelligible only where or to the extent that it is disclosed vis-à-vis an ontological antecedent (something ultimately more fundamental than *our* world/order) coinciding with what we could call absolute indetermination. Boethius takes pains to keep world and God distinct from each other, without alienating them from one another. How is this achieved? By presenting the production of the world in terms of *verbum*, divine mind/thought manifest in speech. Through the divine "verbal" articulation of the divine as *law* (grammatically, a "name" related to the Greek *nomos*), our world is at once tied to God and independent of it. Our world may then be seen as an *answer* open to a fundamental *question* (the providential nature to which Cicero dedicated a "dangerous" dialogue that medieval Christians could still read, if only secretively, as guide into thinking about the divine).[2]

Doctrines retracing our world to a divinity via emanation ought to specify that emanation entails mediation, albeit a unique one, without which the divine would remain utterly opaque to our understanding, but also completely alien to human affairs and concerns. Hence Boethius's insistence upon characterizing God's free will in terms of a *verbum* that "produced the heavens and created earth, so as to establish worthy natures from heaven as celestial dwelling and so as to compose earthly things from earth." The establishment of "worthy natures from heaven" (*dignas coelo naturas*) as well as the composition (Boethius writes, *componeret*) of earthly things (*terrana*) results directly from the *verbum* as "free will" of the "divine nature" that "freely wanted to shape world/order" (*sponte mundum voluit fabricare*). What does the forging of order entail? It entails the establishment of worthy natures from heaven and the assembling of earthly things. The Word "brought/led forth" (*pruduxit*) the heavenly dwelling of the "worthy natures" it thereupon established (*efficeret*). The heavenly "worthy natures" were established on their heavenly seat, the *place* brought forth by the Word. Where is that place prior to the Word's bringing it forth? Let us provisionally bracket this question to return to the earthly, which is "created" rather than "established." The earth was created as product of art presupposing the heavens including their *natures*. The creation of the earth *as a whole work of art* would then seem to presuppose *natures* brought forth into the heavens by the Word (where the distinction between heaven and earth evokes the one between nature and art). Did those "worthy natures" abide elsewhere prior to the Word "raising" them to the heavens? Are we to read Boethius's words in the light of Cicero's *Somnium Scipionis* where heroes are raised to the heavens as divine natures, or stars?

The creative agency of the Word follows the natures brought forth by the Word. Where were those natures *originally*, if not on earth? Were they in the Word itself? Yet, prior to manifesting itself in the willful act of establishing order (*mundum fabricare*), the Word is hidden in the divine mind (or intelligibly in the divine nature). Does the Word draw worthy natures to the heavens from the recesses of the divine mind? Why? To serve as *models* for the art of creating earth (*terram creare*), whence the assembling of earthly things?

If the World is to be intelligible, or be exposed to the divine mind, then it requires mediation: the act by which it is established is not brutal, but gently ordered. Primordially, it involves the forging of order, where there is none. Why? Because outside of God there can be no order. Or rather, there can be no order without intelligence as ordering principle. What is left without order is, by definition, chaos. Not, to be sure, an obstacle to God's free will, which is "omnipotent" in the strict sense that God can do all that he wants, not that he wants *anything*. His power is not infinite in a "mortal" sense, but in the sense that it is *complete*, or "infinitely perfect," resting as it does in his will to order. So the order itself is not extrinsically infinite: the universe is finite within God's infinite mind. Otherwise God would simply think his own infinity. Yet, he cannot think himself if not in, as and through a determination. Yet, God does not want what he cannot do; his will is not compelled by anything to reach out beyond his will. Why? Because all there is outside of God falls ontologically short of God (and, as the classics taught, what is high does not seek what is low). As "matter" vis-à-vis mind.[3]

## Notes

1 See Soars 2020's sensible advice: "Before we too quickly assume . . . that the Christian doctrine of creation *ex nihilo* is the paradigmatic example of a metaphysics of causality in which the effect (the world) is *not* ontologically existent in its cause and

that, therefore, creation *ex nihilo* must be diametrically opposed to any sort of notion of emanation *ex deo*, we would do well to remember that disjunctive binaries tend to divert attention away from the subtler conceptual convergences and disagreements in seemingly opposed systems by forcing their basic premises into preconceived schemas" (952).

2 The dialogue in question is, of course, the *De natura deorum*, which Aquinas would have known formally via the likes of the Bishop of Hippo. See Ward 2015; 307–26.

3 On the meaning of "omnipotence" referred to God's Will, see Andreacchio, Jan. 25, 2022.

# 15 Creation and the Problem of Omnipotence

Misunderstanding the classical sense of "omnipotence" leads logically to a misunderstanding of divine agency. Divine omnipotence is perfectly compatible with the existence of a chaos, or "hell" outside of God. This "outside" that is no negation of God—no absolute absence of the divine—is a "place" in which God's Word is lost, or rather abandoned. This is the lesson inherited by Dante and echoed in the very first Canto of his *Inferno*, but confirmed in the last where we are shown that the loss of order entails primordially a betrayal of the Word or free will that stems directly from the mysterious recesses or eternal being (Boethius's *eternum*) of the divine nature. This nature is immutable, as Aristotle would agree, in the respect that it moves without departing from itself. Hence Boethius's *ex . . . in* clause: the divine's nature does not alter as it comes out of itself to return within itself. This is possible only if it remains itself between the two "moments"—between Alpha and Omega. But this is the case where the Alpha and Omega are conjoined by divine brings free will, or where the divine "extends" in an act that bridges its departure and its return.[1] But why would the divine depart from itself? To establish order out of disorder; to own its shadow. The nature of eternal being is such that being extends over what betrays it, what distances itself from it in betrayal. Being fills the distance with its free act, intervening everywhere, reaching out to the betrayer himself, even though, "as the light shines in the dark, the dark does not grasp it" (τὸ φῶς ἐν τῇ σκοτίᾳ φαίνει, καὶ ἡ σκοτία αὐτὸ οὐ κατέλαβεν—John 1:5, anticipating 3:19). The Vulgata reads, *lux in tenebris lucet: tenebrae*, the dark recesses of hell, of the place of betrayal of light, are, notwithstanding themselves, filled with light. Light reaches out within their abyss, whence traditional depictions of Christ descending into the underworld, world of shadows (compare Acts 2:24 and Ephesians 4:10).

Thus is the abandoning of freedom filled with freedom, while the love of the Father fills the distance separating him from his Prodigal Son, even as the Father has not created the place of or for betrayal—for false freedom. Why, the Father's own perfection precludes his overcoming the dark. Not only does the dark not overcome the light; neither does light overcome the dark. The dark shadow of the divine Word cannot be grasped once and for all. Thus

DOI: 10.4324/9781003405689-16

must hell remain a bottomless pit and its flames *as if* eternal. For they follow perpetually from the free and complete governing act of eternal being. Indeed, the ordering presupposes darkness (and vice-versa) as its substratum, not as an obstacle that the divine will attempts to dispel in itself, but as "material place" for ordering—an ordering that begins, as Boethius shows, with the transposition of "worthy natures" into the heavens where they may serve as models for the creation of earth, and so for earthly art as the art of making wholes (as a child can assemble clay figures) or earthly composites.

## Note

1 In Augustine's *Confessions*, Book 10.20, God is the alpha and omega of memory, as of the universe of discrete contents of human consciousness (where a remembrance is a surfacing-determination of the imagination, as sign that the human mind uses to rise back into its divine perfection).

# 16 Logos as Key to Creation

Somehow mirroring heaven, Boethius's earth is a place for creation, for *art*, nature's imitation. The Word would create earth in the respect that it would determine it as a whole and this act of determination or consolidation would serve as prototype for the assembling of earthly things (*terrena*). In the cited Boethius passage, *creatio* may then be rendered best in terms of "consolidation." Earth is consolidated based on the place in which worthy natures are first transposed, as divine models, out of the divine nature via its Word. In Platonic terms, the "divine natures" will be the Ideas or eternal forms of all things modeled upon and thus participating in them, if only through the Word allowing us to contemplate divine forms, or the forms of the divine mind, in the heavens above the earth.

Where do the foregoing considerations leave us with respect to the Christian doctrine of *creatio ex nihilo*? While the passage cited from Boethius opens with an appeal to the free will of the divine nature *singulare tantum*, the author introduces that will only in the act of leading us to its identification with the *word*, the *logos*. Logos/*verbum* is the key bridging the gap between *pure* being and being in a derivative sense, to echo the formulations of the medieval *Liber de causis*, so important for Aquinas himself.[1]

While in Latin translations of the Proclean/Plotinean "Book of Causes" (*Liber de causis*, hereafter *LDC*) we find free will as mediating God and "everything else," in the apparently-original Arabic version of the *LDC*, as Richard Taylor noted, "the language of emanation is present and directly connected with *abda'a* (*creare*) on the part of *al-mubdi'* (the Creator) (though) no discussion of will, choice or decision is found."[2] In the *LDC*, "creation" is presented as *de facto* emanation, when it comes to intellect, and as an act mediated by intellect when it comes to anything else "created."[3] In other words, all things aside from intellect and divine being itself are "created" intellectually. But how can the divine "create" intellectually if not in the respect that intellect reaches out of itself, or manifests itself in speech, as *verbum*? Boethius's formulations answer our question.

Taylor's own conclusion about the *LDC* confirms that a non-philosophical reading of :

Creation" in terms of "volition" is ultimately inadequate. In Taylor's words, the author of the *LDC* presents an "apparent conflation of the philosophical notion of *ibdii'* and the religious notion of creation in the context of the project of introducing philosophical principles and reasoning developed from Proclus and Plotinus into the cultural and developing scientific context of Islam in Ninth century Baghdad.

(Taylor 119)

Indeed, medieval theology as a whole is pervaded by the scholarly effort to read a pre-philosophical sense of creation in *intellectual* terms—an effort that can succeed only in and through the *verbum*. For falling short of the Christian Word, "creation" negates all freedom, whether 1. by being read in terms emanation in which the created is absorbed directly in the creative act, or 2. by being conceived as an act in which creatures could not possibly participate actively and thus, too, where the creature's innermost *being* would be contradicted by and risk falling into *utter nothingness*, insofar as the creature's own being would depend entirely upon a cause alien to the being's own freedom (which would thereupon be *eo ipso* negated).

Taylor does not face the question of the Word as key to understanding the problem of divine will.[4] Showing that "Divine freedom of will and the possibility of a refraining from emanative creative causality is not found in the *LDC*," Taylor establishes the *LDC* in the tradition of "Neoplatonism" that extends at least from Plotinus to al-Farabi and Avicenna, all of whom would present the primary mode of causality, or the act of the First Cause, as being immediate and thus independent of any act of will or willful deliberation (128, 131).

Taylor does note that Chapter 22 of the *LDC* invokes intelligence as means for divine governance of all that is "below" or dependent from intelligence, yet, as Taylor further notes, the *LDC* stresses that God's *direct* governance overrules and overshadow the one mediated by intelligence, since "nothing whatsoever escapes" God's governance (133–34). Hence the absence of references to a divine will or choice in the *LDC*, suggesting that divine creation is to be understood in terms of *emanation*.

Why then would High Middle Ages readers of the *LDC*, first and foremost St. Thomas Aquinas, speak of creation in terms of a divine will? Does Aquinas depart from the *LDC* in spite of himself or notwithstanding his professing no such departure? A simple and negative answer is invited by three considerations: 1. for Aquinas, the divine will is none other than divine intellect insofar as this presents itself in a theological-political context; 2. Aquinas agrees with Boethius in seeing the Word as key to a proper understanding of the distinction between divine and human will; and 3. when read in the light of Boethius, the *LDC* allows for human freedom as participation in divine necessity.

Taylor quotes Aquinas's relatively early *Commentary on Lombard's Sentences* (*In Sent.*) as agreeing with "the philosophers" that "creation out of nothing" implies that what is created does not owe its being to anything other than the divine mind, be this "other" another creature or another creator.[5] This is precisely the point Boethius has made. Yet, Aquinas adds that philosophers cannot demonstrate that something is created *in time*— as if being and non-being were temporally incompatible, as if *all* order had a beginning in time, or as if there had ever been a time prior to time's own beginning. An Augustinian consideration, to be sure, that Aquinas sees as opening the door to faith. For it is through faith alone that we can see creation in time.[6] Thus in asking "whether the 'university' of creatures began" (*utrum universitas creaturarum incoeperit*), Aquinas finds confirmation, not only in the testament of faith in a divine will creating all things *ex nihilo*, but in Aristotle himself, that there is no rational necessity to any beginning in time; which is to say that there is no absolute beginning of the duration of the totality of beings.[7] In other words, the absolute beginning of "the totality of created beings" (the *universitas creaturarum*) is not simply generated, as if there were any duration prior to the absolutely beginning,[8] or as if there were some empty place, or vacuum predating the order that is the universe (*nos autem dicimus non fuisse locum aut spatium ante mundum*).[9] For the beings constituting the order we call world are produced together with their own "material" time and motion (time being the measure of motion)—"in God, who produces at once the form and the matter" (*in Deo, qui simul producit formam et materiam*).[10] Yet, it is reasonable to speak of the universe as beginning in time insofar as this way of speaking is conducive to knowledge of divine creative power (*manifestius . . . mundus ducit in cognitionem divinae potentiae creantis, si mundus non semper fuit, quam si semper fuisset*).[11] To proclaim that our natural world has a beginning in time is to invite reflection on that world's source, or on the essential nature of causation, rather than taking all order for granted—as an opaque answer to all possible questions. Yet, the source of our world cannot be something other than what Aquinas calls God, namely the absolute plenitude of the being (*esse*) of all beings (*entium*), where God is *being* in and of itself (*ipsum esse per se subsistens*); for assuming that the motion of the universe, or of the total order of beings, arises at some point in time, that "moment" or "now" (*nunc*) cannot precede the motion of things, insofar as time is a function of motion, as Aristotle himself reminds us.[12] And so the teaching that the universe's duration has a beginning points directly to the divine creative act, or to the emanation of duration in and of itself out of eternal being (where *ex nihilo* entails *ex deo*, as Soars reminds us.[13]

In sum, Aquinas shows that the total order of beings (*entium universitas*) is eternal in God, even as we are inspired to appreciate the eternity of Order/World by trusting (hence the appeal to *fides*) poetic accounts of the beginning of all order, or more precisely the (biblical) account that testifies to the absolute dependence of all motion and order upon a timeless source.[14]

## Notes

1. On the importance of the *Liber de causis* in Aquinas, see Taylor 2012 (viewable at https://core.ac.uk/download/pdf/213075095.pdf).
2. Taylor 2012: 118. Taylor will later confirm that "the vocabulary of will (*iriidah* and related terms) does not appear in the *LDC*" (134).
3. In Book 3 of the *LDC*, we read that "the first cause created the being of the soul via intelligence" (*causa prima creavit esse animae mediante intelligentia*) where—as we read in Book 4—being is "the first of created things" (*prima rerum creaturarum*), even as the first cause is itself "pure being and one" and intelligence is "the first created entity" (*ens creatum primum*), though it is "second" with respect to "the first creating entity" (*ens primum creans*) and where the First Cause is *creans omnes res*: creative of all things. Clearly intellect is not "created" in the same sense that all other created things are *through* intellect.
4. For Tyler, "precisely how the author of the *LDC* would have dealt with the issue of divine will and free creation or even whether it would have been a concern to him has to remain an unknown matter of speculation" (134).
5. *In Sent.*, Book 2, d. 1, Q. 1, Art. 2, resp.
6. *ST*, I, Q. 46 ("Of the Beginning of the Duration of Created Things"—De principio durationis rerum creatarum), Art. 2 ("Whether it is an article of faith that the world began"—*Utrum mundum incoepisse sit articulus fidei*). On Maimonides's stressing the philosophical or rational senselessness of divine creation in time, see Seeskin 2012, esp. 197. In his *Guide*, Maimonides effectively shows that Plato's "creation *de novo*" (*huduth*)—entailing the essentially timeless character of the primal mode of creation of every finite being—is compatible with a biblical notion of creation *ex nihilo* (Seeskin, *ibid.* after *Guide* 2.30).
7. *ST*, I, Q. 46, Art. 1, resp.
8. *Ibid.*, resp. to obj. 3.
9. *Ibid.*, resp. to obj. 4.
10. *Ibid.*, resp. to obj. 6.
11. *Ibid.* and 7.
12. *Ibid.*
13. Soars 2020.
14. Though, on the face of things, the opposition between philosophy's eternal world and biblical creation is fundamental or radical, by its very nature thought pierces surfaces, transcending opinions to enter into the vital cradle of intelligibility. Thus can we ask as regards the eternity of the world in God and creation as coinciding with the agency of eternal ideas. Creation could then emerge as the proper work of a "pure consciousness" that is one with the constant interaction between forms of intelligibility. On Maimonides's breaching the wall separating philosophy and the Bible on the question of creation, see Green ed. 2013: 70. Green highlights Strauss's reminder that Maimonides comes as far as to speak of "philosophers who teach creation from nothing" (77). While these strange philosophers remain nameless, they shift the battle-front away from the question of creation, inviting the supposition that the real dividing line between philosophy and the Bible is marked by the question of special or humanly-visible providence, as opposed to a providence affecting the "general" order of things, but that is as blind to human specificity as is unaided Law (78–79). Yet, again, Maimonides readily makes allowance for philosophical recognition of particular providence. The discussion will consequently shift to the question concerning the nature of particular providence, leading us to face a conflict formalized under the banners of intellectualism and voluntarism. And here Maimonides takes a definite stance in favor of "excellence of intellect" to be "dispersed through society as much as possible" as necessary condition for the restoration and preservation of civil freedom (79).

# 17 The Essence of Human Freedom

Creation "from Nothing" as Divine Intellective Emanation

Evidently, Aquinas does not invoke any "creation from nothing" in the sense that God transformed a "non-being" into a "being." In Andrzaj Maryniarczyk's words, "the theory of *creatio ex nihilo* does not mean that being was called into existence 'out of non-being,' but that the Creator is the cause of everything that is."[1] On the contrary, Aquinas and his theological brethren read creation in fundamentally *philosophical* terms, indeed in line with a Platonic tradition that had, itself, rejected any reduction of world/order to anything other than the Good itself.

Yet, a close reading of our medieval authors suggests that there is no fundamental contradiction between the early-Church "philosophical" doctrine that *ex nihilo nihil fit*, or that nothing arises out of nothing, and a later "theological" doctrine that all things come *ex nihilo*, or "out of nothing." Aquinas helps us see beyond any such contradiction, showing us that both doctrines are aspects of one and the same *philosophical*, or more precisely Platonic, intuition.

Aquinas's cutting of the Gordian knot that has long twisted doctrines to make a trap for literalists, is most notable in what the *doctor angelicus* has to say about the bond tying God and our world. How are we to understand the act of creation in itself?[2] Aquinas is prompt to admit that that act is, in itself, eternal. It is its eternity that calls to naught the reading of creation *ex nihilo* as entailing a "temporal" or "sequential" passage from non-being to being. It is only in the eyes of men, or more precisely materialists (thus non-Platonists), that God converts non-being into being, or that the divine will decides/determines, seemingly irrationally, that what is not should be. In reality, the "absence" of a son prior to the son's birth is *accidental* to the birth. Similarly, God's engendering "a being" (*ens*) is independent of anything other than God himself. The engendered, determinate being may be "new" for anyone other than God, but not for God, out of whom and back to whom the being "flows." Accordingly, Aquinas stresses that in the divine will, cause and effect/result coincide, whether they are necessary or not, that is, whether we consider them in themselves or with respect to "proximate causes." The divine will acts immediately, rather than through any deliberation. Yet divine necessity *discloses* freedom and in that respect is free, for freedom is a kind of extension of necessity. Yet, again, freedom is not found in sheer contingency or lack of necessity, but in man's natural reasoning, which responds to divine necessity by gathering proximate causes back to a first cause, the only "inexhaustible" cause that can have "exhaustible" effects or products. Thus does Aquinas write:

> The divine will is to be understood by intellect (*intelligenda*) as existing outside of the order of beings, or as some cause out of which flow a being as a whole and all of its differences. But there are differences between a possible and a necessary being; and so from the divine will itself are originated necessity and contingency in things and the distinction between the two is grounded in proximate causes; for it disposed necessary causes for the effects it wanted to be necessary; but for the effects it wanted to be contingent, it ordered causes acting contingently, i.e., capable of exhausting themselves. And according to the condition of these causes, effects are said to be either necessary or contingent, though, if you will (*quamvis*), all depend upon the divine will, as upon a first cause that transcends the order of necessity and contingency. But this cannot be said of human volition, nor of any other cause; for all other cause falls under the order of necessity or contingency; and thus it must be that either the cause itself exhausts itself, or the effect is not contingent, but necessary. But the divine will is inexhaustible; yet, not all effects are necessary, for some are contingent.[3]

Human freedom does not determine its end or itself, insofar as man is determined as a free agency. Our freedom is our life as mandate to gather the contingent unto a divine necessity (to "render it to God" as in Mark 12:17) in the light of which the contingent acquires meaning, rather than being merely negated, or silenced. Man's freedom makes sense of the contingent by exposing it to the necessary forms of pure intelligibility.

To objectors, Aquinas responds:

> I answer saying that we have free choice with respect to things that we do not want by necessity, or by natural instinct. For that we want to be happy does not depend upon our free choice, but upon our natural instinct; whence other animals that are moved by natural instinct to something are not said to be moved by natural choice. Thus it is with God wanting his own goodness out of necessity, but other things not truly out of necessity . . . with respect to those things that he does not want out of necessity, he has free choice.[4]

What does this tell us about the act of divine creation? That act is primarily not an act of "free choice," but it involves free choice in the respect that it discloses it *in man*. Through man, divine necessity acquires the character of free choice, insofar as man is called to respond, which is say to choose freely the good that is not a given necessity for man as man; for he *is* (i.e., he has his being) to the extent that he *chooses* the good, or to return to it. Thus, God is free through man-in-his-essence, otherwise acting out of strict necessity; and man is free through God, by being called to order the contingent in the light of intelligible necessity.

Boethius himself calls us to ask if or how divine eternity is reconcilable with physical mortality. How can eternity and time, as divine necessity and human freedom, both *be*? Cast in epistemic terms, how is God's knowledge compatible with human freedom? How can God know *human* things, as opposed to things that are "always?" How, in short, is divine providence possible? How can God stoop down from his eternal throne to attend to merely human, not to speak of all-too-human matters? Why would they matter to him, in the first place? What would their significance be in the mind of God?

## Notes

1 Maryniarczyk 2016: 240.
2 Though inviting recognition of the "free" character of divine "emanation"—beyond any split "between *necessary* emanation and *free* creation"—Soars 2020: 958–60 falls short of addressing the problem of mediation between God and World, or rather between the absolute indetermination of Being and determinate being(s); by the same token Soars does not come fully to terms with the question of divine creation as pertaining fundamentally to the absolutely original sense of *causation* in which artistic "making/creating" coincides with natural "generation/evolution."
3 "*Similiter ex parte voluntatis divinae differentia est attendenda. Nam voluntas divina est intelligenda ut extra ordinem entium existens, velut causa quaedam profundens totum ens et omnes eius differentias. Sunt autem differentiae entis possibile et necessarium; et ideo ex ipsa voluntate divina originantur necessitas et contingentia in rebus et distinctio utriusque secundum rationem proximarum causarum: ad effectus enim, quos voluit necessarios esse, disposuit causas necessarias; ad effectus autem, quos voluit esse contingentes, ordinavit causas contingenter agentes, idest potentes deficere. Et secundum harum conditionem causarum, effectus dicuntur vel necessarii vel contingentes, quamvis omnes dependeant a voluntate divina, sicut a prima causa, quae transcendit ordinem necessitatis et contingentiae. Hoc autem non potest dici de voluntate humana, nec de aliqua alia causa: quia omnis alia causa cadit iam sub ordine necessitatis vel contingentiae; et ideo oportet quod vel ipsa causa possit deficere, vel effectus eius non sit contingens, sed necessarius. Voluntas autem divina indeficiens est; tamen non omnes effectus eius sunt necessarii, sed quidam contingentes*" (Aquinas, *De Interpretatione* ["Of Interpretation"], Book 1, Lecture 14.22).
4 "*Rispondeo dicendum quod liberum arbitrium habemus respectu eorum quæ non necessario volumus, vel naturali instinctu. Non enim ad liberum arbitrium pertinet quod volumus esse felices, sed ad naturalem instinctum; unde et alia animalia, quæ naturali instinctu moventur ad aliquid, non dicuntur libero arbitrio moveri. Cum igitur Deus ex necessitate suam bonitatem velit, alia vero non ex necessitate . . . respectu illorum quæ non ex necessitate vult, liberum arbitrium habet.*" *ST*, I, Q. 19: "Of the Will of God" (*De Voluntate Dei*), Art. 10 ("Whether God Has Free Choice"—*Utrum Deus habeat liberum arbitrium*), sc.

# 18 Eternity and Dialogue

The answer to all of the foregoing questions is univocal in our age of disenchantment with eternity: there is no eternity to begin with, but only a divined *power* at work in the course of Evolution. Maybe the power is conscious, as we might be when attending to our daily affairs, but it is not conscious in the way the Platonist Boethius would argue God is, which is to say, binding the temporal to the eternal, or physical being to its purely intelligible archetype. Such a binding-activity would involve both the inherence and transcendence of the divine vis-à-vis the human. Hence the importance that Aristotle is awarded by later Scholastics. For Aristotle had articulated Platonic teachings in such a way as to respond to the suspicion that the eternal was not present in the temporal, or that *special* divine providence was impossible. How can the divine be involved in properly human affairs, as opposed to the constant motion of the heavens where the orientation of "the arrow of time" is of little or no significance? That "arrow" matters to *us*. And so *our* God must be conscious of it, which is to say that his thought(s) must be eminently capable of discriminating between birth and death, between right (and the righteous) and wrong, between good and evil (and the wicked), between true and false. In short, God must be present in human *freedom*; he must thus be *living*, as opposed to being *merely* eternal. But how can this be? Boethius's Platonic answer is *Logos*, the Word. God is living in and as Logos, Discourse, or more precisely Dialogue, a Reason that binds (hence the *dia-* or "across" of "dialogue") eternal being to physical being and vice versa (both sides of the coin are needed to establish and sustain order/world).

The living Logos shows us that we are not lost in physical motion, but that physical motion is to be understood in the light of eternal being, the immutable. Logos tells us that the body is nothing but a shadow of mind, yet not of a mind blind to the body, but of one that gathers its shadows, as a shepherd his flock, back towards itself into an order, a world (*mundus*/κόσμος) established for the purpose of exposing mortal shadows to immortal Gods—the shadows' "resurrection" in eternal being.

Logos would then be the founder of our world, the order in which bodies reflect pure minds, minds unfettered by bodies. Logos emerges as dialogue between the bodies and their original inherence in eternal being, as minds. Logos exposes and in exposing redeems fallen, broken or corrupt being. For in Logos, eternal being is present in mortal being as providential agency.

What salvation does the Living Word offer? That of exposure of "sin"—of crime, of fault, of abandonment, of betrayal—to our original condition, our "proper place" beyond any physical compulsion. There is no escape from compulsion, from false freedom, outside of dialogue rooted in eternal being, our own being outside of deception, prior to our forsaking the eternal. Why has the eternal forsaken the temporal or physical? Because the physical has forsaken its immutable "parent." Yet, in Logos the physical partakes in the noetic, the purely intelligible, being allowed to separate itself from the stream of compulsion otherwise condemning bodies to perpetual strife.

In sum, Logos is key to Boethius's (and Aquinas's) account of the divine and *is*, in a significant respect, that very account. For in speaking, Boethius is not representing any personal "viewpoint" or "opinion"; nor is he reasoning in a Cartesian fashion, as an ego/individual cut off from divine providence. In speaking, Boethius is awakening to his own eternal being. To echo St. Paul, we may say that it is Logos itself that is speaking in Boethius and in speaking as it does, Logos is exposing Boethius' physical being to the divine.

Does God see the properly human? Yes, in Logos, God's living presence in *freedom*. Is the body as such free? No. Are we free? What *are* we? As long as this latter *anthropological* question is not addressed, it is senseless to answer the former. *What* are we? If we are free, then

what is that which is free? Boethius's answer, of course, is: the divine will, disclosed as God's Logos, which is active in the establishment of all order, as in the ordering of all physical being.

Are there shadows outside of the presence of God in Logos? Yes, even as they depend upon God's eternal being. The eternal has a perpetual shadow. Call that shadow, "matter" (ὕλη). God does not "create" it (what could it possibly mean to "create one's shadow," nay the very shadow of the creative act?).[1] Yet, he *orders* it and indeed, properly speaking, there is no Chaos or absolutely undifferentiated matter to be spoken of, aside from God. For in speaking we partake in the Logos that orders Chaos, the perpetual shadow of God. To face Chaos *as such*—Chaos as absence of world—we would have to abandon all Logos, the faintest trace of speech. We would have to betray dialogue, altogether. That is *hell*, which God does not create; as he does not create the evil entailed by the abandonment of Logos for the sake of entering into God's shadow *as if it were* God's own mind. This is precisely what Eve appears to be doing in the Garden of Eden. The reptilian voice she hears is a dark echo, a "vocal shadow" of the voice Eve cannot hear upon distancing herself from Adam.[2] That primal voice is the one reverberating outside of the Garden as the presence of Logos in the abysmal recesses of the divine mind; yet that same voice speaks well within the Garden itself as *law*, or in terms of the *names* Adam is at least in part familiar with.

Boethius's God enters into the human as that which is most properly human, namely Logos, the speech that establishes order—that forges a world, a *mundus*—out of God's own perpetual, underlying shadow. Boethius's eternal mind is, then, not at all incompatible with freedom, as modern scholarship is apt to conclude.[3] For we are free to the extent that we are called or "elected" (*ego elegi vos*, reads John 15:16), drawn into the Logos, into dialogue with eternal being. Our very identity is shaped by the Living Word and outside of it we cannot be free, but must fall back into that shadow so vividly described by the expression, "hell's fire."

## Notes

1  In Book 13.33 of his *Confessions*, St. Augustine speaks to God concerning his works (*opera*), noting: "they are made by you out of nothing, not out of you, but not out of something that is not yours or that was there earlier, but out of a matter concreated—which is to say, simultaneously created by you—a matter whose informity you formed without any temporal interposition" (*de nihilo . . . a te, non de te facta sunt, non de aliqua non tua vel quae antea fuerit, sed de concreata, id est simul a te creata materia, quia eius informitatem sine ulla temporis interpositione formasti*). While the Bishop's *"non de te"* ("not out of you") suggests that God's works are not made of God's own substance—which entails an original, perfect coincidence of matter and form—the *matter* out of which God's works are said to be made is created *simultaneously* with its form by an immediate act of formation. The doctrine of creation "from" (*ex*) nothing would then suggest that the matter and form of things arise simultaneously "from" (*ex*) God as absolute source, *without subtracting* anything from God, as the expression *de Deo* would otherwise suggest. In sum, time and space would not define the proper context of finite beings. That context could be ultimately nothing other than God himself. Creation must then be "originally" good or perfect in God, and "fallen" only through an *agency* inferior to, though deriving from God's own.

2  The biblical account warrants the proposition that evil is a permanent "empty possibility" in which man can fall, thereby losing or degrading his being—his heroic mandate—within it, even as man's fall is accompanied *simultaneously* by God's providential calling/gathering of man back to the divine integrity of his being, which is to say, to his being in God. In bringing light into the dark, or in imitating Lucifer, man would then carry with him, if only unconsciously, the *active function* of light. In "stealing" the fire of the Gods, Promethean man would be bringing with him God's own *intention* (inherent in the fire), which would at once mysteriously turn man's betrayal in the service of God.

3  Exemplary is Helm 2009, which misses entirely the role of *verbum* in Boethius's account (itself, evidently, a mode of *verbum*) of God.

# 19 Medieval Teachers of Freedom

What is freedom? Who is free? For Boethius freedom is divine and we are free only to the extent that we rise in the divine, *trusting* the divine call raising us out of the dead, as Ephesians 2:8–9 reminds us when it notes that salvation comes through faith, or διὰ πίστεως, "not from work" (οὐκ ἐξ ἔργων), as if salvation depended upon man's own power, or any power other than God's own, where power is bound to divine intelligence. But now, what is salvation? What does it mean to be raised out of the dead? For Boethius this raising must be one out of the underworld, the realm of shadows, whereby we rise to awareness of our twofold condition. For Logos draws us out of a place among shadows, into our place among eternal beings. In Logos the two places *coincide*:[1] we are at once permanently hidden in God's shadow and eternally revealed in God's light; abiding, as Dante showed most vividly, at once in Limbo and in Elysian Fields.

The freedom both Aquinas and Boethius defend is, evidently, constantly rooted in God via his providence, which comes to fruition in our own providence, our own freedom as heroic return to God via the contingencies of life. The human being finds himself in a dangerous place, called to face danger by *being* dangerous. Danger is a *calling* and we are called to face it by being given the ability to respond to the heart of all danger, truth itself. It would be ludicrous to establish our heroism, our being-dangerous, in terms of autonomous individuality, as we see done in the modern world at least ever since Kant invoked his "as if" ideals to justice what would be known as "the march of History," namely a world established on the principles of modern/progressive mechanistic science. There is something fundamentally reprehensible in the contemporary appeal to God as *means* to "re-enchant" our societies in the wake of a "death of God" that our institutions—not least of them our schools—accept to the point that they take it thoughtlessly for granted. Either God is a political-theological calling, or he is a pet, a stuffed animal we use to justify our "killing" him in our everyday lives, where "killing God" means living in fundamental denial of divine providence, or betraying divine agency in our search for truth and thus in our daily "practical" speech. Once we accept the modern severing of political/public speech from the challenge of divine intellection, God is *de facto* dead for us. We then abide in God's death, in the *shadow* of God that is traditionally designated by the term "hell."

With our medieval writers, God is not an ideal used to make a fundamentally meaningless existence bearable, but the source of our freedom that explodes the mechanistic universe of modernity to expose its fallacy, namely the mistaking of human natural ends (and so too of the proper end of our reason/discourse) as the product of human ingenuity, a product we are to build and realize in the future. The Deistic habit to appeal to God *ex machina*, as a useful "ideal" (the type of distraction Nietzsche dubbed "idol") in our struggle to "deny death," is altogether incompatible with our medieval sources and their logos, their heroic response to a divine calling. That calling, for them, comes through intellect manifest in a discourse or reason gathering the contingent *back* into a mysterious intelligibility. An at once rational and poetic journey is involved, here; one whereby mind/thought (*mens*) orders its world back into God, to paraphrase the title of a work by a renowned contemporary of Aquinas.[2] In Platonic terms, as human beings we are called to "imitate" the natural act by which the divine generates all things. In rendering unto God what God bestows upon us, human art imitates its divine prototype.

The foregoing considerations suggest that the root of the discrepancy between Aquinas and modern Thomism pertains to the status of volition, most notably with respect to intellection. On our present reading, while speaking formally on behalf of theology, Aquinas speaks as a philosopher at heart.

## Notes

1. The ambiguity of the coincidence at hand is highlighted by Dante in Canto 4 of his *Inferno*. See Andreacchio 2013a.
2. Cf., St. Bonaventure's *Intinerarium mentis in Deum* ("Journey of the Mind into God").

# 20 The Philosophical Heart of Medieval Scholarship

Aquinas's ultimately Platonic-philosophical reading of divine volition is reflected in the Proem to his *In Sent.*, Book 2, where the distinction is stressed between philosophical and theological ways to consider creatures. "For philosophers consider creatures according to that which they are constituted of in their own nature; whence they inquire into the proper causes and passions of things;[1] but the theologian considers creatures insofar as they exuded from a first principle and are ordered back into an ultimate end that is God." At a first glance, Aquinas appears to speak as a theologian, for he indicates that the "second book" under consideration treats of "things' origin, the act of the principle itself and the effect of the act" (*rerum principium, principii ipsius actum, et actus effectum*).[2] Yet, when we explore further Aquinas's reading of divine creation in terms of *direct emanation* from God via a "will" read, in turn, as intellective extension of God, we are reminded of Aquinas's formal depiction of Plato's conception of creation as merely demiurgic: in moving formally beyond Plato, Aquinas is returning to Plato or a Platonic/philosophical understanding of divine creation in terms of the fundamental sense of generation. Here creatures arise directly out of eternity (*ab eterno*), "created" by the light, "as the sun emits its rays" (*sicut sol radios suos emittit*), insofar as creatures are "participations" in the light (*participationes sui, diffundit [sol] ad rerum creationem*), *determinations* of divine light. The light in question is what the biblical tradition, no less than the Platonic, refers to as "spirit" (*spiritus*)—conventionally spoken of as "will" (*voluntas*)—which has the "power" or "hand"/*manus* (to speak biblically) to reach from eternal being to temporal or physically determined being: "they who wished to shorten this hand are those who have construed that nothing can be produced by God out of nothing" (*Hanc manum abbreviare voluerunt qui a Deo nihil fieri posse ex nihilo astruxerunt*). The doctrine of creation *ex nihilo* is then, for Aquinas and in harmony with the classical-medieval tradition of Platonic philosophy, a doctrine about the intimate relationship between human freedom and divine necessity, whereby the two interpenetrate *intellectually*. Aquinas's articulation of the problem of freedom is unequivocally Platonic/philosophical, presenting divine volition as property of divine intellection, thereby avoiding what, philosophically speaking, is the pitfall of voluntarism.[3]

Philosophy proper objects to voluntarism insofar as our natural reason (*ratio naturalis*) objects to the primacy of will over intellect, a primacy whence would follow the obscuring of dialogue between man and God.

Where God's agency is imagined in terms of an impulse at work outside of the "flow"/emanation of divine intelligibility into human providence (*viz.*, virtue, prudence, justice, etc.), God is *eo ipso* presented as threatening at any moment to rupture the bond between virtue and knowledge.[4] In Platonic terms, the conceptions involved here are mistaken and misleading, based as they are on a nominal/hypothetical reduction of divine knowledge to its human correlative. For the philosopher who has let go of all human prejudices, exposing his own determined being to absolute indetermination or divine necessity, divine knowledge is not a fixed certainty negated by freedom, but a living word or *logos* binding man's "strength of mind" (*virtus*) indissolubly to an eternal order of things that is not susceptible to any alteration or mutation. Divine knowledge is an intellect providing constant support to live rationally even in this life, when we are exposed to the temptation of taking a "volitional leap," thereby facing faith (*fides*) in voluntarist terms—not as trust in the goodness of the eternal order of things in God, but as belief in what breaks through all immutability to establish the primacy of freedom over necessity. Now, for the philosopher as philosopher this voluntarist move is uncalled for, based as it is on lack of patience, or rather care for what is eminently given *in principio*. Philosophy awaits the voice of God speaking through man's own voice to guide us back to our *proper* or *natural place* (to speak with Aristotle), where Man and God are mysteriously and luminously one. The "place" in question is disclosed by a *graceful* (civil and peaceful) act that is both creative and good, both just and eminently desirable.

It is in turning to this "original place" of harmonious conversion between God and man that the philosopher asks if the divine creative act constitutes an impenetrable barrier between the human and the divine, or if it does not rather disclose indissoluble dialogue between the two poles. For Aquinas and his philosophical friends, Law itself—eternally solemn, concrete face of divine volition—will not be an impregnable, unintelligible fortress, or infernal Door thereto,[5] keeping us safe from truth as the greatest danger of all, while allowing us to build our own fortresses, towers of safety, "democratically" cut off from any real or uncompromising concern with truth proper. On the contrary, Law will be properly or originally a mirror of truth, a *poetic* lens in which we are called to respond to truth, a "spectacle" producing life as direct participation in truth itself. Likewise, the divine will shall not be conceived as holding divine truth at bay as terminal threat to the stability of our own authority, our own arcana, or the "negative infinity" of our own self-righteousness, our own perpetually-hungry sense of entitlement.

## Notes

1 "A being is the proper object of intellect and as such it is the first intelligible thing" (*ens est proprium objectum intellectus, et sic est primum intelligibile—ST*, I, Q. 5, Art. 2, sc.
2 *In Sent.*, Book 2, Prologue.
3 See Bourke 1964: 83. On this problem, particularly as it pertains to the distinction between Aquinas's reading of Bernard de Clairvaux's *De Gratia et Libero Arbitrio* ("On Grace and Free Choice") and St. Bonaventure's correlative reading, characterized by greater emphasis on volition, see Cuff 2018: 38–41. Cuff provides an ample bibliography on the subject of the nature of volition in Christian theology.
4 On the providential character of prudence as well as on the very prudential character of providence in Aquinas, see Torrell 2008; esp. pp. 95–96 of Ch. 2 "'Dieu conduit toutes choses vers leur fin.' Providence et gouvernement divin chez Thomas D'Aquin" (republished from *Miscellanea Mediaevalia*, 29 [2002], Berlin, pp. 561–94), pp. 63–97.
5 See Dante, *Inferno* 3, 1–18.

# 21 The Problem of Voluntarism

In standing unequivocally for the primacy of intellect over will—where the latter emerges as authoritative face of the former—Aquinas's Platonic tradition responds to the voluntarist tendency to strangle dialogue under the sway of mechanically imposed dictates.[1] If God's *decisions* are utterly opaque to our understanding, then on what grounds should we object to the decisions of all-too-human authorities? If the ultimate or divine sense of causation is defined by volition *beyond* intellection, then why should our own "sciences" not attempt to couch our intellection in irrational or *mechanical* impulses?

Voluntarism opens the door to the *mechanistic* conception of natural causality characteristic of our own natural sciences and shared by and large even by their religious opponents. Accordingly, today's by far most prominent objection to the modern doctrine of Evolution takes the shape of "Intelligent Design" theories attempting to carve a niche for God in a technocratic Leviathan feeding off of what the nineteenth century proclaimed as the death of God. Indeed, the dominant trend of our mechanistic age is to conceive everything and everyone *ex machina*, in an "objectified" manner. In the context of our globally mass-mediated rhetorical habits, God himself is both appealed to or rejected as a "god from the machine" that, either way, does not disturb in the least our currently hegemonic mechanistic conception of nature.

Not accidentally has it been in Protestant circles that Intelligent Design arguments have found their most outspoken heralds. For, given its relative marginalizing of classical Platonism—read most notably through Aristotle—with respect to Catholicism, from its very inception Protestantism has exposed itself to serve as mouthpiece for modern modes of discourse, or the modern voluntarist attempt to read intellection *progressively* as a function of volition (whereby a new "intellect"/science arises on unintelligible/"material" grounds).[2] Nevertheless, contemporary Thomists do not fare much better than their relatively-submissive Protestant colleagues, since, even when refusing to tread in the shadow of Teilhard de Chardin (for whom divine creation is evolving towards a future perfection), today's neo-Thomists tend to rely on a mechanistic reading of nature, even as they abide in eager anticipation of the discovery of "scientific" evidence of the irreducibility of form to

DOI: 10.4324/9781003405689-22

matter (thereby rejecting the Darwinian "evolutionary" reduction of essence to genealogy).[3]

Yet, the discrepancy between Aquinas and modernity's evolutionism pertains to questions that modern "natural science" fails to ask, let alone try to answer—questions about the essential constitution of experience, the relation between bodies and speech, or even the *original* character of the interaction between form to matter. How is *artistic* creation, including the formulation of "scientific" doctrines—not least of them, that of Evolution—to be understood vis-à-vis *natural* generation?

Taking his bearings from the consideration that "Augustine distinguishes the work of propagation, which is the work of nature, from the work of creation" (*Augustinus . . . distinguit opus propagationis, quod est opus naturae, ab opere creationis*), Aquinas concludes that "creation is not admixed with the operations of nature, but is presupposed by the operation of nature" (*in operibus naturae non admiscetur creatio, sed praesupponitur ad operationem naturae*).[4] The argument leading to this conclusion pertains ostensibly to the ontological status of form as "concreated" (*concreata*) as the Aristotelian "potentiality" of a being. The form of a being (of an *ens*) does not subsist aside from matter, but *is* that which matter always is, insofar as matter without form would not *be*.[5] The form of a being is not the product of nature, insofar as "what arises out of a natural agent is a composite, which arises from matter" (*Quod . . . proprie fit ab agente naturali, est compositum, quod fit ex materia*).

In responding to a "fourth objection," Aquinas adds that "there is no operation of nature unless it presupposes created principles and so those (beings) that arise by nature are called creatures" (*operatio naturae non est nisi ex praesuppositione principiorum creatorum, et sic ea quae per naturam fiunt, creaturae dicuntur*). Thus, natural generation pertains to material composition defined by "forms" that are "concreated" for their respective material determinations with respect to which forms act as governing principle or *providential presence* of the divine in nature.[6] The forms and their "matter" are mutually irreducible, both being concreated directly out of their divine *unity*. Yet, the matter is dependent upon form, as the bodily-inanimate is as upon soul. Thus God is properly and directly the source of form/soul and only indirectly or secondarily of the physical. Hence Peter Lombard's stressing that God "created the substance of the soul in which [the body] could live: not out of some matter, be it corporeal or spiritual, but out of nothing" (*substantiam animae in qua [corpus] viveret, creavit: non de materia aliqua corporali vel spirituali, sed de nihilo*), *that is*, directly out of God himself.[7] Thereby the soul seeks to gather its own physical or bodily motion back into God, even as it must fail to succeed without divine aid. What the soul can achieve—that is, what it does relatively to itself—"in this world" is the *government* (or moderation) of bodily motion in the light of an original divine unity of form and matter in which matter coincides with God himself as " 'material cause' of the world."[8] Yet, relatively to God, the soul's own agency is necessarily, indeed providentially aided by God's creative act, in which matter is originally fully gathered in form, thereby constituting a perfect, eternal order, divine archetype of all human or political order.

Lombard's God, just as Aquinas's, is constantly at work in generation, not as a mere material-like power—be it mechanically immanent or mechanically transcendent—but via divinely-created forms governing material motion as motion that arises *informed* to begin with. The forms in question are not, to be sure, created out of pre-existing material motion; rather, they arise as the "defining limits" of motion itself, out of God himself and thus by an act that is ultimately at once creative and generative. For the act of creation is primordially that of the divine emptying itself into an intellective act (represented most notably by the second person of the Trinity) through which all beings arise and in which all things are gathered (the term *intelligere* suggesting literally a "reading/binding within," as in Aquinas's *intus legere*).[9]

## Notes

1 On the voluntaristic roots of modernity, see MacIntyre 1981, Lutz 2008 and Murchadha 2022.
2 See Strauss 1965: 58–61, where Strauss concludes that "Puritanism, having broken more radically with the 'pagan' philosophical tradition (i.e., chiefly with Aristotelianism) than Roman Catholicism and Lutheranism had done, was more open to the new philosophy than were the latter. Puritanism thus could become a very important, and perhaps the most important, 'carrier' of the new philosophy both natural and moral—of a philosophy which had been created by men of an entirely non-Puritan stamp." Though addressing strictly Puritanism in the context of a discussion on Max Weber, in the context of the conflict between Athens and Jerusalem, Strauss's argument applies to Protestantism as a whole vis-à-vis Catholicism.
3 For an attempt to reconcile Thomism with Intelligent Design theories, see Chaberek 2017. For a more radical exploration of the limitations of evolutionism, see Andreacchio, July 6, 2022. For a recent bold, if only exuberant effort to expose contradictions in the doctrine of evolutionism (cf., chicken-or-egg impasse), see Edwin Wright's arguments at https://planegeodesy.com/appendix-i-creation-and-the-method-of-saint-thomas-aquinas#fnref15 and https://planegeodesy.com/appendix-ii-evolutionism-refuted-by-the-ribosome#fnref1. Alternatively, some scholars have sought to defend Intelligent Design by aligning it to ancient pagan myths about demiurges, as if the biblical God were an agent presupposing an Idea of the Good outside of himself. See for instance Jaffa 2006.
4 *ST*, I, Q. 45 ("Creation"—*Creatio*), Art. 8 ("Whether creation is admixed with the operations of nature and art"—*Utrum creatio admisceatur in operibus naturae et artis*), resp.
5 "The form of the natural body is not a subsisting being, but that which something is" (*forma naturalis corporis non est subsistens, sed quo aliquid est—ibid.*).
6 On Aquinas's defense of the immanence of God's intellective act in sensory perception, see Jolivet 1935: 184–85. Unfortunately, Jolivet upholds Aquinas's lessons on metaphysics merely *formally*, as hypotheses in need of being assessed in the context of a presumed "historical evolution" of conceptual/intellectual positions (188). Unlike modern "intellectual historians," Aquinas refuses to abstract form from matter if

only with the intent of establishing a *new* universal/scientific form resolving within itself all matter, *a posteriori*.
7 Lombard 1841, Book 2, Dist. 17 (*De Creationae Animae*—"Of the Creation of the Soul"), Ch. 1.
8 Soars 2020, 956.
9 Cf. *In Sent.*, Book 3, Dist. 23n Q. 3, art. 1; and *De Veritate*, Q. 15, Art. 1, sc. 7. On *intelligere*, see also Vico 2013, Book 2: "Of Poetic Wisdom" (p. 97). In the modern world inaugurated most notably by Machiavelli, nature and art are supposed to fuse "historically" into a technological world "beyond good and evil." The key discrepancy between 1. the classical divine *coincidentia* of generation and creation, and 2. its modern "historical/progressive" counterpart pertains to the nature of mediation. Whereas, in the modern case, "unity" is established *mechanically* through alienation from "origins" (reflected in ancestral Tradition), in the classical case, generation and creation are one only ontologically prior-to and beyond all mechanical reproduction. The classical *metaphysical* unity of generation and creation is replicated, in own Age, in terms of a neo-Romantic "creative imagination" (redolent of Nietzsche's "appropriation" of Christian or "esoteric" Platonism) expressed in the medium of technology. For a witty articulation of the problem at hand, see Peter Kreeft, "10 Lies of Contemporary Culture," Commencement Address at the Franciscan University of Steubenville, delivered on May 14, 2022, uploaded on June 1, 2022 at www.youtube.com/watch?v=K7FtUlnIXd0&t=759s.

# 22 From Intelligent Design Back to Platonism

Contrary to what contemporary Thomists are apt to suggest, the incompatibility between Aquinas's lesson and modern "Intelligent Design" theorists is not limited to the former's *de facto* rejection of any "god of the gaps" intervening *ex machina* to explain our failure to account for natural diversity in strictly mechanical terms.[1] Aquinas's incompatibility with modern biology is radical, insofar as the medieval Platonist-at-heart rejects *any* mechanistic reading of natural mutation, including the "scientific" one that modern Thomists accept if only by blessing it with an ecclesiastical *nihil obstat* granted in anticipation of a return, namely popular approval of the glorious authority of a God justifying modern Thomists.

For Aquinas, diversity in nature is to be understood in terms of *divine emanation* via an intellective act and so in terms of a divine "gathering" of determinations into divine, absolute indetermination. The return of all "physical" determinations into God's own absolute indetermination is entailed by emanation's intellective character, whereby the divine creates in terms of *formae mentis*, "intellective forms" ordering all finite emanations into "organisms" (wholes) reflecting God—each to the degree allowed, as Aristotle had taught, by their respective place within the greater Whole of Being itself. There is then no "evolution" from one species to another, but "emanation" of species in the context of a whole spectrum of emanations that run their course, as it were, in function of a terminal emanation, namely "Adam," the human being as such, a being fully reflecting the divine *coincidentia* of generation and creation, or art and nature.

The hiatus between species remains a divine mystery entailing an abyss of unquantifiable intelligence. For Platonists what separates one species of beings from another can be nothing other than the intelligent ground of all origination/emanation, where emanation orders a world with diverse species interacting in the interest of *one* species through which all others are "returned" to the source of both their being and consciousness. Evidently, that species is the human one, the species of beings naturally or spontaneously prone to ask questions, or to "convert" all given answers into questions, or mirrors of intelligible origins.[2] The human being as such, or his *moral-poetic* agency, emerges, then, as unique key to the constitution of distinctions between species of beings. Accordingly, for our medieval authors, the key to understanding life is not any mechanistic "biology," but a poetic art that is one with our own life well lived as we participate in the divine coincidence of art and nature. For then we ourselves convert into artistic creations, yet not ones that reduce natural generation to serve ends alien to it, but ones reflecting ends at the heart of generation.

The alternative to the poetic immediacy implied by the doctrine of "creation from nothing" is a *machine* or a materialist reading of generation for which a mechanism is supposed to explain the distinction between producer and product, marking the impossibility of any *dialogue* between the two. Freedom, in this case, is impossible or absurd, which is to say reduced to compulsion. Thus, on a mechanistic reading of "emanation" (production, or generation), the classical distinction between natural generation and artful creation disappears. The two are conflated into a "mechanical nature," as generation is reduced to a mechanism devoid of consciousness, or vis-à-vis which consciousness can be no more than a contingent super-structure. This is the view that is dominant in the modern world, or on the basis of early-modern conceptions of nature (cf. Machiavelli, Galileo, Spinoza, Hobbes, etc.).

Unlike ancient materialists or those whom Aristotle would call "philosophers of nature," early-modern materialists do not limit themselves to reducing human freedom to natural necessity. Instead, they attempt to establish a novel *synthesis* of freedom and necessity, a "scientific" one that is supposed to overcome medieval "sacred poetry" in terms of clinical precision and clarity, thereby *realizing* empirically what medieval discourse promises for the afterlife. Modern materialism raises necessity to the status of freedom, presenting nature as *evolving into human freedom*. Freedom is then a natural *compulsion*. This account of or "solution" to the problem of freedom led to the manifest political-theological or ethical-metaphysical crisis of the twentieth century; until we reach our own day, where the rise of technology as consummate *deus ex machina* eclipses all talk about a crisis in the *institutionalizing* or *normalizing* of "crisis." Today, there is no crisis because crisis is the "new normal" and the original dialogue between man and God is replaced by feelings and opinions about God as a neo-Kantian hypothesis we use or reject for the sake of making life, our everyday dying, bearable in the absence of the *living* God, Father of all fathers, intelligible essence of all generation.

The death of God is most evident not in any outright rebellion against an absolute mode of causality, but in the relativizing of all causality via a conceptual reduction of all causes to mediated or secondary ones. Necessarily, God's creative agency is denied by those who retrace anything involved in the production of anything else to a first cause other than God. Just as the artisan's art is predicated on a natural foundation, so too will that foundation presuppose a first cause other than itself. But what is other than both artists and nature itself must be God, artisan of nature itself; yet not in the sense that

God needs to look at another nature to produce the nature serving as support for human nature, but in the sense that God produces nature out of himself, or out of his own resources. God, in other words, gives of himself to produce nature, just as man gives of himself to produce his artifact. Yet, while man presupposes something outside of himself, God presupposes what is within himself. And since nothing is outside of God as support for the creative act, it is said that that act is "from nothing," meaning that God does not rely on anything outside of himself. But this does not mean that 1. God does not rely on something within himself (most notably, eternal Ideas), and 2. God *creates* the "negative-place" that he "fills" and thereby determines, and so *orders*, upon creating something. The "negativity" that God "fills" with a being he produces is presupposed by all creation, not temporally—for creation is eternal—but in the respect that it accompanies the act by necessity, as a shadow accompanies a hand. In other words, God's *positive* infinity (his infinite perfection) is permanently mirrored by his *negative* infinity, or the "absence" that God's creative act or presence fills. God cannot avoid the negativity without which the "place" of any being could not be determined.

In Aristotelian terms, divine creation involves a distinction, even division, of form and (material) content, without which human freedom would be impossible. For human freedom stands or falls on an "artistic" effort to order sensory powers within nominal/poetic forms, with the understanding that the effort presupposes an original, now lost unity of form and content. Falling short of that effort, we squander our freedom, which is thereupon replaced by sheer license, namely the "freedom" of the unfree. Yet, how can human freedom thrive in the absence of a providential agency supporting it, or outside of the context of *divine freedom*? The freedom that we exercise in ordering our passions in a human or political Whole, God exercises effortlessly by ordering all beings eternally from within. In presenting God as acting from without the world he creates, our traditional stories invite us to reflect upon origins in human terms. Otherwise put, our stories invite us to discover divine agency at the heart of human agency; divine providence at work within heroic providence. Now, this applies both to biblical stories and to pagan counterparts, not least of these the Platonic *mythoi* that Aquinas must have had in mind when he wrote:

> Ancient philosophers . . . did not consider the emanation of particular effects unless it came from particular causes, for which it is necessary to presuppose something in the emanation's action (as if the emanative act were not free—TN); accordingly, it was their common opinion that nothing arises from nothing. But this does not pertain to the first emanation from the universal principle/beginning of things.[3]

Aquinas is not explicitly addressing the central problem of Platonism, namely that of the original identity of goodness and being. "Ancient philosophers" are reminiscent of Aristotle's pre-Socratic "natural philosophers" or philosophical "materialists"; hermeneutically speaking, "literalists." What is at stake for Aquinas, no less—and no more—than for Plato, is the challenge of transcending reducible or derivative senses of causation, thereby returning to an absolute mode of causation wherein generation and creation are eternally one. Hence Aquinas's further considerations:

> Creation is not mutation unless strictly relatively to a mode of intellection. For in the order of mutation, something remains itself while altering between now and before; for whenever a being is the same in act, it alters between now and before (i.e., it alters in time—TN), as in motions relatively to quality, quantity and place; but sometimes a being is the same strictly in a state of potentiality, as in a state of mutation relatively to substance, whose subject is matter. But in creation, through which is produced the whole substance of things, the same thing cannot be taken that remains itself while altering between now and before, except strictly relatively to the intellect; as in the case where a certain thing that was after having not wholly been, formerly.[4]

In the creative *act* itself there is no separation between cause and effect, between producer and product. The "effect" is retraceable to the "cause" only with respect to *alienation* from the latter; which is not to say that the effect and the cause are essentially identical. For the effect is ontologically alienated from (thereby falling short of) the (divine) cause in and of itself. Thus, while the effect owes its "essence" to its divine cause, it does not possess God's own essence (*non est ex essentia Dei, sed est ex Deo essentia—ST*, I, Q. 41, Art. 3.2). The immediacy of God's creation of "effects" is not, therefore, matched by the effect's effort to return to God. Whereas in the former case, we find absolute ease, in the latter we find effort doomed in the absence of divine aid.[5]

The discrepancy between what the Greeks would call "the way up" (*anabasis*) and "the way down" (*katabasis*) is defined with Aquinas, no less than with Boethius, by an act of causation serving as primarily intellective *and* secondarily judicious "pivot" between beings and their divine source, as between the realm of mortal life and the otherworldly, whether the latter be conceived as *our* "fallen" world, or as its otherworldly dimension.[6] The "divided line" between the two is defined by a divine Word, intellective articulation manifest to mortals in terms of a judging will, or a living authority that "judges" in the proper sense of *jus dicere*, "to say what is right," or "to speak justice."

Although men find themselves judging and reasoning from-without the subject matter of judgment and reason, that subject matter is eternally gathered within the intellective act in whose shadow (*umbra*) our "rational soul" works. The "forms" that are *for us* abstract in God, include their matter, *for God* himself. Those forms are none other than what things are eternally, namely the forms of pure intelligibility that Plato called Ideas. Where are those Ideas? Medieval Christianity answers by appealing to the Bible's God. What is eternally in God, God's very "subject matter," is Platonic Ideas resolving within themselves the empirical alienation of form and content, as of name and body. Aquinas's God would then be primarily the God of Platonic Ideas properly understood; or, more precisely, God would be the *being* proper to Platonic Ideas, or the mode of being that makes Platonic Ideas what they are, as opposed to things partaking in them in time/duration. These *determinate* beings that are not effortlessly-always, must strive to linger; for in duration what is determinate partakes in its eternal indetermination. In Aquinas's words:

> But all things which already have being, naturally love that being of theirs, and preserve it with all their strength; whence Boethius says in the 3rd book of his *Consolation of Philosophy*: divine providence gave to things created from itself this or the greatest cause to linger, so that, as long as they can, they naturally desire to linger. Wherefore you cannot doubt in any possible way that all things that are have a natural appetite for constancy of permanence and avoid destruction.[7]

Determinate being strives (*appetat*), then, although it is only in man that the striving is reconciled with its intellective context; for in man striving turns "back" to God beyond all possible compulsions. For in man alone among beings, appearances are no longer mere answers for our appetite, but questions moderating our appetite in the service of a common good (*utilitas publica*), which is a good determined purely (thus unmixed with material passions) in the light of a divine, supreme good, or *summum bonum*. Yet, questions entail a "rational conversion" of appearances to their cause(s), which represent(s) a mode of negation of its products, insofar as the cause is conceived as preceding its effect. Only in questioning appearances, or by exposing appearances to the problem of causality, do we begin to face appearances as concrete beings (*entia*). Otherwise stated, sensory appearances acquire reality—they are then *really present*—for us only in questioning, or in the medium of speech open to truth as convergence of appearances and what hides behind them. Yet, upon facing *beings*, we expose ourselves at once to the problem of *non-being*, or of nothingness (*nihil*). In asking questions—indeed in desiring knowledge—man discovers death. Thus it is that non-being (*non ens*, or *nihil*) comes to coincide with the object of *rational* desire, or the good as spring of intelligibility.

## Notes

1 For a concise account of *modernist* appeals to St. Thomas, see Tkacz 2007. Tkacz objects to Intelligent Design theorists, not because they leave God out of the *ordinary* constitution of Nature, but insofar as they seek God as intervening in Nature, to begin with. Thus Tkacz writes: "Many who oppose the standard Darwinian account

of biological evolution identify creation with divine intervention into nature. This is why many are so concerned with discontinuities in nature, such as discontinuities in the fossil record: they see in them evidence of divine action in the world, on the grounds that such discontinuities could only be explained by direct divine action. This insistence that creation must mean that God has periodically produced new and distinct forms of life is to [sic] confuse the fact of creation with the manner or mode of the development of natural beings in the universe." For an example of appeals to Aquinas as providing a metaphysical justification to evolutionism, see Tabaczek 2015. For Tabaczek, "the Aristotelian-Thomistic tradition offers . . . a metaphysical foundation of the mechanism of evolutionary changes and a preliminary description of natural selection" (25); as if what we needed, today, was "a metaphysics that serves as a philosophical foundation for evolutionism and the rule of natural selection" (13).

2  On the need for divine intervention for the creation of new species, see Kaiser 2011–12, fourth part: "Evolution and Creation."

3  "*Antiqui philosophi . . . non consideraverunt nisi emanationem effectuum particularium a causis particularibus, quas necesse est prasupponere aliquid in sua actione; et secundum hoc erat eorum communis opinio, ex nihilo nihil fieri. Sed tamen hoc locum non habet in* prima emanatione ab universalis rerum principio" (*ST*, I, Q. 45, Art. 2, resp. 1).

4  "*Creatio non est mutatio nisi secundum modum intelligendi tantum. Nam de ratione mutationis est, quod aliquid idem se habeat aliter nunc et prius; nam quandoque est idem ens actu, aliter se habens nunc et prius, sicut in motibus secundum quantitatem et qualitatem et ubi; quandoque vero est idem ens in potentia tantum, sicut in mutatione secundum substantiam, cuius subiectum est materia. Sed in creatione, per quam producitur tota substantia rerum, non potest accipi aliquid idem aliter se habens nunc et prius, nisi secundum intellectum tantum; sicut si intelligatur aliqua res prius non fuisse totaliter, et postea esse*" (*ibid*.).

5  In Lecture 1.1 of Book 2 of his *Commentary on Aristotle's Metaphysics*, Aquinas reads the Stagirite as confirming that the primary work of philosophy pertains to the way people come to know truth (*philosophia prima considerat universalem veritatem entium. Et ideo ad hunc philosophum pertinet considerare, quomodo se habeat homo ad veritatem cognoscendam*).

6  For a recent exploration of the classical distinction between *anabasis* (ἀνάβασις) and *katabasis* (κατάβασις), see Adluri, ed. 2013. See also Bonnechère and Cursaru, eds. 2015.

7  "*Omnia autem quae iam esse habent, illud esse suum naturaliter amant, et ipsum tota virtute conservant; unde Boetius dicit in III de consolatione: dedit divina providentia creatis a se rebus hanc vel maximam manendi causam, ut quoad possunt, naturaliter manere desiderent. Quare nihil est quod ullo modo queas dubitare, cuncta quae sunt, appetere naturaliter constantiam permanendi, devitareque perniciem*"—*De Veritate*, Q. 21 ("Of the Good"—*De bono*), Art. 2 ("Whether a Being and the Good Convert into Each Other Fundamentally"—*Utrum ens et bonum convertantur secundum supposita*), resp. On the meaning of *suppositum* in Aquinas, see Tamarchio 1998.

# 23 Being and Nothingness

How are we to understand the "nothing" (*nihil*) preceding a being that stems from the good? Aquinas answers by effectively having the "nothing" coincide with the good itself, insofar as the good precedes every determined being, even though, in the course of reasoning, every being comes before its good, which is discovered by examining beings. Yet, being-in-itself—the one that "precedes" all beings created *ex nihilo*, is the good itself, or God.

In appealing to the *LDC*'s proposition that "the first of created things is being" (*prima rerum creaturarum est esse*), insofar as "relatively to reason, (determinate) being precedes the good" (*ens secundum rationem est prius quam bonum*), Thomas binds our natural desire (of the good) to the problem or challenge of knowledge/science, where "being is the proper object of the intellect, so that it is the first intelligible" (*ens est proprium obiectum intellectus, et sic est primum intelligibile*).[1] In not knowing what is good, the honest man turns to beings, investigating *what* beings are (an eminently Socratic endeavor), thereby exposing himself to (the discovery of) a being or a mode of being coinciding with the good itself.[2]

Aquinas writes:

> In causing, the good precedes a being, as the end is before the form; and for this reason, among the names signifying divine causality, the good is placed before the being (*ens*). Furthermore, given that, following Platonists, who did not distinguish matter from privation, they would say that matter is a non-being, participation of the good extends to more things than participation of a being; for prime matter participates in the good as it longs for it; nothing does it long for unless it is similar to itself; yet, it does not participate unless it is posited as a non-being. And so Dionysus says that the good is extended to non-existing things.[3]

The horizon of participation in the good is greater than that of participation in being in the sense that even matter Platonically understood as a non-being (*non ens*) participates in the good, whereas only beings participates in *being per se*. Thus does Aquinas remain a Platonist at heart, reading matter "in and of itself" as uncreated. But what is meant by matter being "privation," or "a non-being" (*non ens*)? Is that not what, in biblical terms, is otherwise called evil? Beyond "chaos" as "confusion of seeds" (according to etymology), the notion of formless matter seems to imply an abysmal "place" that is indeed uncreated, but that serves as "negative stage" for divine creation. Be that as it may, Aquinas does not in the least contradict a subtle reading of Plato given which matter in and of itself is uncreated or not contained within an idea, but con-caused, as the necessary shadow of creation. Thus we read that,

> according to some, Plato posited matter as uncreated and so he did not posit the being of an idea of matter, but of a con-cause of matter. But since we posit matter created by God, not however (a matter) without form, matter does indeed have an idea in God, yet not apart from the idea of a composite. For matter in and of itself neither has being, nor is knowable,

*(Plato, secundum quosdam, posuit materiam non creatam, et ideo non posuit ideam esse materiae, sed materiae concausam. Sed quia nos ponimus materiam creatam a Deo, non tamen sine forma, habet quidem materia ideam in Deo, non tamen aliam ab idea compositi. Nam materia secundum se neque esse habet, neque cognoscibilis est).*[4]

Aquinas is evidently content with the proposition that both the form and matter of beings are eternally contained in God, with the implication that the divide between form and matter is not absolute. What Aquinas argues against is the notion that matter exists independently of form. If the forms of things, or "things themselves" (their "essence") are eternal in God's mind (i.e., intellectively in divine being), there they must resolve material motion within themselves. In other words, divine ideas are no abstractions from matter. Platonists can then agree with the Bible's creation story insofar as it implies the derivation of *all beings* from a single "substance" in which form and material content coincide. In creating heaven and earth God would be "creating" *order* outside of himself in the sense that he would be *manifesting* an order eternally hidden in God himself.

On the contrary it is said in Genesis 1:1:

> In the beginning God created heaven and earth; (where objectors claim that it is impossible for God to create from nothing outside of himself) I respond saying that not only is the creation of something by God not impossible, but it is necessary to assume that all things have been created by God, as is held in the premise. For wherever someone makes something from something (else), that from which he makes is presupposed by his action and is not produced by the same action, just as the artisan operates from natural things, as from wood and brass, which are not caused by the action of art, but are caused by the action of nature. And yet that same nature causes natural things with respect to form, but it presupposes matter. If

therefore God did not act unless (he did so) out of some presupposition, it would follow that that presupposition would not be caused by himself. But it is evident above that nothing can be in beings that is not in God, who is the universal cause of being as a whole. Hence it is necessary to say that God produces things to be from nothing.[5]

## Notes

1 *ST*, I, Q. 5 ("Of the Good in Common"—*De bono in communi*), Art. 2 ("Whether with Respect to Reason the Good is Prior to a Being"—*Utrum bonum secundum rationem sit prius quam ens*), resp.
2 "Thus it was that the intent of philosophers was principally to attain to knowledge of first causes through all that they considered in things" (*philosophorum intentio ad hoc principaliter erat ut, per omnia quae in rebus considerabant, ad cognitionem primarum causarum pervenirent*)—*In Sent.*, Book 2, Proem.
3 "*In causando, bonum est prius quam ens, sicut finis quam forma, et hac ratione, inter nomina significantia causalitatem divinam, prius ponitur bonum quam ens. Et iterum quia, secundum Platonicos, qui, materiam a privatione non distinguentes, dicebant materiam esse non ens, ad plura se extendit participatio boni quam participatio entis. Nam materia prima participat bonum, cum appetat ipsum (nihil autem appetit nisi simile sibi), non autem participat ens, cum ponatur non ens. Et ideo dicit Dionysius quod bonum extenditur ad non existentia*"—ibid.
4 *ST*, I, Q. 15, a. 3, ad. 3.
5 "*Sed contra est quod dicitur Gen. I, in principio creavit Deus caelum et terram. Respondeo dicendum quod non solum non est impossibile a Deo aliquid creari, sed necesse est ponere a Deo omnia creata esse, ut ex praemissis habetur. Quicumque enim facit aliquid ex aliquo, illud ex quo facit praesupponitur actioni eius, et non producitur per ipsam actionem, sicut artifex operatur ex rebus naturalibus, ut ex ligno et aere, quae per artis actionem non causantur, sed causantur per actionem naturae. Sed et ipsa natura causat res naturales quantum ad formam, sed praesupponit materiam. Si ergo Deus non ageret nisi ex aliquo praesupposito, sequeretur quod illud praesuppositum non esset causatum ab ipso. Ostensum est autem supra quod nihil potest esse in entibus quod non sit a Deo, qui est causa universalis totius esse. Unde necesse est dicere quod Deus ex nihilo res in esse producit*" (*ST*, I, Q. 45, Art. 2, resp.).

# 24 Evil

In its primary sense, matter is uncreated and unknowable, just as is evil. Thus Aquinas's *Summa Contra Gentiles*, Book 1, Chapter 71 ("That God Knows Evil Things"—*Quod Deus cognoscit mala*) ends with the conclusion an evil being is knowable only to the extent that it partakes in, or retains *being*, which is good (*quantum habet de esse, tantum habet de cognoscibilitate*). What is knowable is what matter or evil falls short of and that is, ultimately speaking, God himself as fundamental knower. Knowledge is primarily of divine or perfect being that knows itself primarily and everything falling short of himself insofar as it partakes in divine perfection. Accordingly, *ibid.*, Chapter 48 ("That God knows primordially and inherently only himself"—*Quod Deus primo et per se solum seipsum cognoscit*) confirms that "what is primordially and inherently understood by God is nothing other than his own substance" (*id quod est primo et per se intellectum a Deo, nihil est aliud quam sua substantia*). Intelligence is fundamentally the act by which being gathers itself within itself eternally, or without any movement or mutation—*sine aliqua mutabilitate*, to speak with Boethius, and thus "without being subject to the very possibility of falling short of itself, or of departing from itself, or of falling into *evil*."

Aquinas is in full agreement with the Platonic tradition and most evidently St. Augustine, in thinking of evil as "the privation of some particular good" (*privatio alicuius particularis boni*—*De Malo* ["Of Evil"], Q.1, Art. 1 ["If evil were something"—*An malum sit aliquid*], resp.): "evil, inasmuch as it is evil, is not something in things, but is the privation of some particular good in something particular" (*relinquitur quod malum, secundum quod est malum, non est aliquid in rebus, sed est alicuius particularis boni privatio, alicui particulari bono inhaerens*); again, "that which is evil is not something, but that which happens to be evil is something inasmuch as evil deprives only of a particular good, just as that which is blind (i.e., blindness as such—TN) is not something, but something that happens to be blind is something" (*id quod est malum non est aliquid, sed id cui accidit esse malum est aliquid, in quantum malum privat nonnisi aliquod particulare bonum, sicut et hoc ipsum quod est caecum esse non est aliquid, sed id cui accidit caecum esse est aliquid*). In this respect, evil is a "void" separating beings from the fullness of their being, which is God. That "void" is a "nothing" that is, at once, filled by God. Evil amounts, then, to an *alienation*, even an estrangement rather than to a departure from God. As blindness for the blind, evil is not something in itself, but a condition affecting a being, not insofar as the being *is*, but insofar as the being falls short of *being*, or of the *act* proper of the good itself. Yet, Aquinas states that, "we must conclude that evil does not have an inherent cause" (*relinquitur quod malum non habeat causam per se*). The alienation from God may be called an "accident" of creation, which is *in itself* timeless, as Augustine himself would emphasize.[1] Evil would then be a *permanent* accident of the divine act—just as the unintelligible, uncreated *matter* implied in the notion of creation *ex nihilo*.

**Note**

1 See for instance Augustine's *Confessions*, Book 13.29.

# 25 Creation and Platonic Ideas

What is the matter *created* by God? It is a "composition" of elements (viz., fire, wood, water, iron, earth), rather than their "negative" substratum, without which all material composites would be created directly within God. But the world we live in is a fallen one. Where has it fallen in? What makes it "negatively" possible for the world to "fall?" What "empty place" hosts the composition of empirical material? That "empty place" is the uninformed matter that is not created by God, being, as it were, God's own shadow, or the shadow of God's eternal agency.

On the other hand, it is important for Aquinas to stress that the good that the biblical tradition personifies as God the Father is not a mere Demiurge standing before ideas to mold what, after Aristotle, we would call a "material cause." The cosmological tale of the *Timaeus* presents causality "piecemeal" in various distinct parts. Yet Platonists-at-heart, including Boethius and Aquinas, are primarily concerned with causality in its fundamental unity, or as "first cause." Aquinas's God, as Plato's "idea of the good," is not a mere poetic persona, or a Demiurge, but the "hidden" (sacred/secret) truth about the Demiurge, even as with the Bible what is hidden is boldly proclaimed. Even less, however, is Aquinas's God what he "becomes" in our modern age, namely a "useful value" standing outside of eternal ideas and thus of pure intelligibility, shut to any living dialogue with the human. The contemporary "revival" of God as ideal or value is a petty deception by which the global marketplace of "everything and everyone" feeds even the boldest proclamation of truth to technology as unquestioned master of our "latter days." In short, "God as value" is a pernicious means to promote obscurantism.

What alternative do our medieval scholars propose? God as Father of Ideas, cradle of Intellect by which we are called to be God's own heroes. Thus in Q. 15 ("Of Ideas") of *ST*, I, Plato's ideas as generative and epistemic forms of all things (and thus of experience) are *in* God as eternal intellect, as opposed to standing outside "on their own" (*per se*), or outside of mind.[1] The question is thorny, however, as is the question of the relationship between Zeus, Father of Gods, and all other Olympian Gods. Do the other/lesser Gods exist outside of, or within their Father? Is mind only one idea (form of intelligibility) among others, or is the idea of all ideas a "first question" presupposed by and encompassing all others, if only eternally, rather than temporally? Surely Zeus *is* prior to his *becoming* Father. To follow Plato's transposition of Homeric terms into impersonal ones, or terms that empty their personality in thought itself, we ask: what is mind prior to being thought as a creator acting "in the beginning of time?" Beyond the vulgar or "physical" conception of origins as lost in the past, the Platonist rises to the challenge of discerning origins as an eternal, ever-present source of life.[2] This is where the Father comes to be spoken of even as God-Head, or less controversially as *mysterium fidei*. The idea of all ideas as good generating all things is no mere demiurgic *persona* playfully spoken of in the *Timaeus*.

One could sensibly argue that Aquinas had not read Plato's *Republic* and so that, in presenting the Greek, he was forced to nail him to the Letter of a *mythos*. But Aquinas knew better than to cut any Letter off from its hidden Spirit. He was perfectly capable of recognizing that good friends can hide behind masks before which alone it is fair to say, *magis amica veritas*. For truth hides, just as the good itself, behind the tales of both classical and medieval "antiquity."

## Notes

1 See *ibid.*, a. 3 sc., where, "the Ideas were posited by Plato as principles of the cognition of things and of their own generation" (*ideae a Platone ponerentur principia cognitionis rerum et generationis ipsarum*).
2 In Q. 15, a. 1, ad. 1, Aquinas refers to "Plato's opinion about ideas, following which he posited them as existing on their own, rather than in intellect" (*opinio . . . Platonis de ideis, secundum quod ponebat eas per se existentes, non in intellectu*).

# Bibliography

Adluri, Vishwa, ed. *Philosophy and Salvation in Greek Religion* (Religionsgeschichtliche Versuche und Vorarbeiten, Vol. 60). Berlin and Boston: De Gruyter, 2013.
Albertus Magnus, St. *Super Dionysium De Divinis Nominibus*. Münster: Aschendorff, 1972.
Alston, William P. *Perceiving God: The Epistemology of Religious Experience*. Ithaca and London: Cornell University Press, 1991.
Andreacchio, Marco. "Autobiography as History of Ideas: An Intimate Reading of Vico's Vita," *Historia Philosophica: An International Journal*, 11 (2013): 59–94.
———. "Christianity and Philosophy in Dante," *Mediaevalia*, 42 (2021): 143–86.
———. "Dangerous Thoughts: The First Act of Shakespeare's Julius Caesar," *Voegelin View*, at https://voegelinview.com (April 26, 2022).
———. "Dante's Status and Christianity: A Reading of Purgatorio XXI and XXII in Their Poetic Context," *Interpretation: A Journal of Political Philosophy*, 39.1 (2012): 55–82.
———. "Dante's *Vita Nuova* and Petrarchismo," in *The Routledge Anthology of Anglo-Italian Renaissance*. London: Routledge, 2019: 55–74.
———. "Humanisme et mystère dans la philosophie de Pic de la Mirandole," *Dogma: Revue de philosophie et de sciences humaines*, 14 (2021): 8–38 (Winter 2021).
———. "Introductory Notes on Aquinas's The Will of God," *Voegelin View*, at https://voegelinview.com/introductory-notes-on-aquinass-the-will-of-god/ (January 25, 2022).
———. "Leaving the Technological Cave," *Voegelin View*, at https://voegelinview.com/leaving-the-technological-cave/ (February 2, 2022).
———. "Mastery of Nature," *Interpretation: A Journal of Political Philosophy*, 45.2 (2019): 223–48; and 45.3 (2019): 427–54.
———. "Politics and Women in Shakespeare's *Julius Caesar*, Act 2," *Voegelin View*, at https://voegelinview.com (April 27, 2022).
———. "Redemption: The Third Act of Shakespeare's Julius Caesar," *Voegelin View*, at https://voegelinview.co (April 28, 2022).
———. "Saving Superman: A Daunting Lesson from Old Christianity," *Voegelin View*, at https://voegelinview.com/saving-superman-a-daunting-lesson-from-old-christianity/ (Jan. 6, 2021).
———. "The Bankruptcy of Evolutionism," *Voegelin View*, at https://voegelinview.com/the-bankruptcy-of-evolutionism/ (July 6, 2022).

———. "The Ideology of Transparency: Creating the New Sodom and Gomorrah," *Voegelin View*, at https://voegelinview.com/the-ideology-of-transparency-creating-the-new-sodom-and-gomorrah/ (September 23, 2022).

———. "The Inverted Order of Things: Shakespeare's *Julius Caesar*, Act 4," *Voegelin View*, at https://voegelinview.com (June 15, 2022).

———. "The Triumph of Rome: Act 5 of Shakespeare's *Julius Caesar*," *Voegelin View*, at https://voegelinview.com (June 22, 2022).

———. *Trans-Modernism: Genesis of a Horror Scene*, at www.youtube.com/watch?v=j0uW9uGPNfY&t=70s (September 14, 2022).

———. "Unmasking Limbo: Reading Inferno IV as Key to Dante's Comedy," *Interpretation: A Journal of Political Philosophy*, 40.2 (2013a): 199–219.

Aquinas, Thomas St. All works cited from www.corpusthomisticum.org/iopera.html: *Commentary on Aristotle's Metaphysics* (*Sententia libri Metaphysicae*), *On the Eternity of the World* (*De Aeternitate Mundi*), *On Truth* (*De Veritate*), *On Interpretation* (*De Interpretatione*), *On Spiritual Creatures* (*De spiritualibus creaturis*), *Commentary on Lombard's Sentences* (*Scriptum super Libros Sententiarum Magistri Petri Lombardi*), *Commentary on Aristotle's Ethics* (*Sententia Libri Ethicorum*), *Summa contra Gentiles Summa Theologiae Commentary on the Gospel of John* (*Super Evangelium S. Joannis Lectura*), *Exposition of the Book of Causes* (*Super librum De causis expositio*).

Augustine, St. *City of God* (*De civitate Dei contra paganos*), at www.augustinus.it/latino/cdd/index2.htm.

———. *Confessions* (*Confessiones*), at www.augustinus.it/latino/confessioni/index.htm.

Averroës. "Aristotelis Stagiritæ Metaphysicæ libri XII Cum Averrois Cordubensis Commentaris," in *Aristotelis Opera cum Averrois Commentaris* (Venice: Junctae, 1562). Frankfurt am Main: Minerva, 1962.

———. *Decisive Treatise and Epistle Dedicatory* (Translated with an Introduction and Notes by Charles E. Butterworth). Chicago: Chicago University Press, 2001.

Barrow, John D. and Frank J. Tipler. *The Anthropic Cosmological Principle*. Oxford: Clarendon Press, 1986.

Bittle, Celestine N. *From Aether to Cosmos*. New York, Milwaukee and Chicago: The Bruce Publishing Company, 1946.

Blondel, Maurice. "Histoire et Dogme: Les lacunes de l'exégèse moderne (1904)," in Blondel, M, ed., *Oeuvres Completes* (Vol. II). Paris: PUF, 1997.

Boland, Vivian. *Ideas in God According to Saint Thomas Aquinas*. Leiden: Brill, 1996.

Bonaventure, St. "Intinerarium Mentis in Deum," in Regis J. Armstrong OFM trans. ed., *Into God: Itinerarium Mentis in Deum of Saint Bonaventure*. Washington, DC: The Catholic University of America Press, 2020.

Bonnechère, Pierre and Gabriela Cursaru. eds. *Katábasis dans la tradition littéraire et religieuse de la Grèce ancienne. Actes du Colloque de Montréal et de Québec* (2–5 mai 2014, 2 Vols, Les Études classiques, 83 [2015], Special Issue). Namur: Société des Études Classiques, 2015.

Bourke, Vernon J. *Will in Western Thought: An Historico-Critical Survey*. New York: Library of Liberal Arts, 1964.

Bradley, Denis J.M. *Aquinas on the Twofold Human Good: Reason and Human Happiness in Aquinas's Moral Science*. Washington, DC: The Catholic University of America Press, 1997.

Brock, Stephen L. "On Whether Aquinas's 'Ipsum Esse' Is 'Platonism,'" *The Review of Metaphysics*, 60.2 (2006): 269–303.

Burrell, David B. *Aquinas' Debt to Maimonides: A Straight Path: Studies in Medieval Philosophy and Culture: Essays in Honor of Arthur Hyman* (Ruth Link-Salinger, ed.). Washington, DC: Catholic University of America Press, 1988.

Burrell, David B. "Creation and 'Actualism,'" *Medieval Philosophy and Theology*, 4 (1994): 25–41.

Chaberek, Michael OP. *Aquinas and Evolution: Why St. Thomas' Teaching on the Origins Is Incompatible with Evolutionary Theory*. Langley: The Chartwell Press, 2017.

Charles H. Manekin, "Belief, Certainty and Divine Attributes in the *Guide*," *Maimonidean Studies I*, 30.1 (1990).

Cicero. *De natura deorum* ("On the Nature of the Gods," Translated by H. Rackham. Loeb Classical Library). Cambridge: Harvard University Press, 1994 [1933].

Cicero. "Epistles to Atticus," *Book 2*, at www.thelatinlibrary.com/cicero/att2.shtml.

Clarke, Norris. "The Problem of Reality and Multiplicity of Divine Ideas in Christian Neoplatonism," in Dominic J. O'Meara, ed., *Neoplatonism and Christian thought*. Albany: State University of New York Press, 1982.

Cuff, Andrew Jacob. *The Influence of Bernard of Clairvaux's Analysis of Human Freedom on the Cistercian Masters of the Thirteenth and Fourteenth Centuries* (Doctoral Dissertation). Washington, DC: The School of Theology and Religious Studies of the Catholic University of America, 2018.

Cusa, Nicholas of. "De quaerendo Deum," in P. Wilpert, ed., *Opuscula i: De Deo abscondito, De quaerendo Deum, De filiatione Dei, De dato patris luminum, Coniectura de ultimis diebus, De genesi*. Hamburg: Felix Meiner, 1959.

Dante (Alighieri). "Comedy," in Giorgio Petrocchi ed., *La Divina Commedia*. Firenze: Le Lettere, 1994 [1966–67], at https://dante.princeton.edu/pdp/.

———. "Convivio," in *Edizione Nazionale*. Firenze: Le Lettere, 1995, at https://dante.princeton.edu/pdp/.

De Chardin, Pierre Teilhard. *The Phenomenon of Man* (*Le phénomène humain*, Translated by Bernard Wall). New York: Harper & Brothers, 1959.

De Clairvaux, Bernard. *De Gratia et Libero Arbitrio*. Landishuti: Attenkofer, 1842.

DeSpain, Benjamin R. *Thinking Theologically about the Divine Ideas: Reexamining the Summa of Thomas Aquinas*. Leiden: Brill, 2022.

Doolan, Gregory T. *Aquinas on the Divine Ideas as Exemplar Causes*. Washington, DC: The Catholic University of America Press, 2008.

Duhem, Pierre. *Le Système du Monde : Histoire des doctrines cosmologiques de Platon à Copernic* (Tome V). Paris: Librairies Scientifique Hermann et Fils, 1954.

Fabro, Cornelio. *La nozione metafisica di partecipazione secondo San Tommaso d'Aquino*. Roma: Edivi, 2005 [1939].

Forgie, William J. "The Cosmological and Ontological Arguments: How Saint Thomas Solved the Kantian Problem," *Religious Studies*, 31.1 (1995).

Geiger, Louis B. "Les idées divines dans l'oeuvre de S. Thomas," in Armand Maurer et al., eds., *St. Thomas Aquinas 1274–1974: Commemorative Studies* (Vol. 1). Toronto: Pontifical Institute of Mediaeval Studies, 1974.

Gluck, Andrew L. "Maimonides' Arguments for Creation Ex Nihilo in the Guide of the Perplexed," *Medieval Philosophy & Theology*, 7.2 (1998): 221–54.

Gravina, Gian Vincenzo. *Opere giuridiche* (Book 2). Naples: Stamperia di Giuseppe Raimondi, 1757 (Reprinted in Gianvincenzo Gravina, *Della Ragion poetica*. Edited and introduced by R. Gaetano, Soveria Mannelli: Rubbettino, 2005).

Green, Kenneth Hart, ed., *Leo Strauss and Maimonides, Leo Strauss on Maimonides: The Complete Writings*. Chicago and London: The University of Chicago Press, 2013.

Guénon, René. *Le Règne de la Quantité et les Signes des Temps*. Paris: Gallimard, 1972 [1945].

Helm, Paul. "Eternity and Vision in Boethius," *European Journal for Philosophy of Religion*, 1.1 (2009): 77–97.

Henle, Robert John. *Saint Thomas and Platonism: A Study of the Plato and Platonici Texts in the Writings of Saint Thomas*. The Hague: Martinus Nijhoff, 1970.

Hibbs, Thomas S. *Dialectic and Narrative in Aquinas: An Interpretation of the Summa Contra Gentiles*. Notre Dame and London: University of Notre Dame Press, 1995.

Hobbes, Thomas. *Humane Nature, or, The Fundamental Elements of Policy being a Discovery of the Faculties, Acts, and Passions of the Soul of Man from their Original Causes, According to Such Philosophical Principles as Are Not Commonly Known or Asserted*, 1650, at https://library.um.edu.mo/ebooks/b13602317.pdf.

Husserl, Edmund. *The Crisis of European Sciences and Transcendental Phenomenology: An Introduction to Phenomenological Philosophy* (Translated by David Carr). Evanston: Northwestern University Press, 1970.

Israeli, Isaac ben Solomon. "Liber de definitionibus," in *Israeli, Opera omnia Ysaaci*. Lyon [Lugdunum]: Officina Johannis de Platea, 1515, at https://findit-uat.library.yale.edu/bookreader/BookReaderDemo/index.html?oid=10957208#page/7/mode/1up.

Jaffa, Harry. "Who Owns the Copyright to the Universe? Evolution in Itself Reveals an Intelligent Design," *Claremont Review of Books*, 6.2 (2006), at https://claremontreviewofbooks.com/who-owns-the-copyright-to-the-universe/.

Janssens, David. "Introduction to "Plato's Apology of Socrates & Crito," *(accompanying transcripts of Leo Strauss's Fall 1966 Course)*, at https://leostrausstranscripts.uchicago.edu/philologic4/strauss/navigate/19/1/3/?byte=4511.

Jolivet, Régis. "L'intuition intellectuelle et le problème de la métaphysique," *Archives de Philosophie*, 11.2 (1935).

Kaiser, Thomas J. "Something from Nothing This Way Comes," Fourth Part: "Evolution and Creation," *The Aquinas Review*, 18 (2011–2012): 1–33.

Katz, Jerrold J. *Realistic Rationalism*. Cambridge and London: MIT Press, 1998.

Klein, Jacob. *Lectures and Essays*. Annapolis: St. John's College Press, 1985.

Krauss, Lawrence M. *A Universe from Nothing: Why There is Something Rather than Nothing* (With an Afterword by Richard Dawkins). New York and London: Free Press, 2012.

Kreeft, Peter Kreeft. "10 Lies of Contemporary Culture," *Commencement Address at the Franciscan University of Steubenville*, (May 14, 2022), at www.youtube.com/watch?v=K7FtUlnIXd0&t=759s.

Kretzmann, Norman. *The Metaphysics of Creation: Aquinas's Natural Theology in Summa Contra Gentiles II*. Oxford: Clarendon Press, 2001 [1998].

———. *The Metaphysics of Theism*. Oxford: Clarendon Press, 1997.

Langiulli, Nino. "A Liberal Education: Knowing What to Resist," *Academic Questions*, 13.3 (2000): 39–45.

Lombard, Peter. *The Four Books of Sentences (Sententiarum Libri Quatuor), Book 2, 24.5 (De libero arbitrio—"Of Free Choice")—p. 192 of Petri Lombardi Sententiarum libri quatuor.* Paris: Migne, 1841.

Lundy, Steven J. "Varro's *Theologia Tripertita* in Augustus and Augustine," *Paper Delivered at "The Intellectual Legacy of M. Terentius Varro" Session of the SCS Annual Meeting*, January 2015, Unpublished paper.

Lutz, Christopher Stephen. "From Voluntarist Nominalism to Rationalism to Chaos: Alasdair MacIntyre's Critique of Modern Ethics," *Analyse & Kritik*, 30.1 (2008): 91–9.

MacIntyre, Alasdair. *After Virtue: A Study in Moral Theory.* Notre Dame: University of Notre Dame Press, 1981.

Maimonides, Moses. *The Guide of the Perplexed* (Translated by Shlomo Pines, 2 vols). Chicago: Chicago University Press, 1974.

Maryniarczyk, Andrzej. "Philosophical Creationism: Thomas Aquinas' Metaphysics of Creatio Ex Nihilo," *Studia Gilsoniana*, 5 (2016): 217–68.

Matula, Jozef. "Thomas Aquinas and his Reading of Isaac Ben Solomon Israeli," in Alessandro Musco, Giuliana Musotto and Carla Compagno, eds., *Universality of Reason. Plurality of Philosophies in the Middle Ages* (Acts of the 12th International Congress of Medieval Philosophy in the Middle Ages (Palermo, Italy, Sept. 16–22, 2007, Vol. 3). Palermo: Officina di Studi Medievali, 2012.

Millerman, Michael. "On the Literary Character of "The Guide for the Perplexed': Aporia and Euporia," *Interpretation; A Journal of Political Philosophy*, 42.1 (2015).

Moreschini, Claudio, ed., Boetius. *De consolatione philosophiae. Opuscula theologica.* München and Leipzig: K.G. Saur, 2005.

Murchadha, Felix Ó. *The Formation of the Modern Self Reason: Happiness and the Passions from Montaigne to Kant.* London and New York: Bloomsbury Academic, 2022.

Nagel, Thomas. *Mind and Cosmos: Why the Materialist Neo-Darwinian Conception of Nature is Almost Certainly False.* Oxford: Oxford University Press, 2012.

Noé, Jean-Baptiste. *Le déclin d'un monde : Géopolitique des conflits et des rivalités en 2023.* Paris: L'Artilleur/Bernard Giovanangeli éditeur, 2022.

O'Daly, Gerard. *Augustine's City of God.* Oxford: Oxford University Press, 1999.

Owens, Joseph. "Thomistic Common Nature and Platonic Idea," *Mediaeval Studies*, 21 (1959): 211–23.

Pieper, Josef. *The Silence of St. Thomas* (Translated by John Murray and Daniel O'Connor). New York: Pantheon Books, 1957 (originally published as *Philosophia Negativa: zwei Versuche über Thomas von Aquin, Negative Philosophy: Two Essays on Thomas Aquinas*, München: Kösel, 1953).

Plato. *Phaedo* (Translated by Eva T. H. Brann, Peter Kalkavage and Eric Salem. Focus philosophical library). Newburyport: Focus Pub./R. Pullins, 1998.

Posti, Mikko. *Medieval Theories of Divine Providence 1250–1350.* Leiden and Boston: Brill, 2020.

Rahner, Karl. *Nature and Grace: Dilemmas in the Modern Church.* New York: Sheed and Ward, 1964.

Rovighi, Sofia Vanni. *L'antropologia filosofica di San Tommaso d'Aquino.* Milano: Società editrice Vita e Pensiero, 1965.

Schall, James V. "On Postmodernism and the 'Silence' of St. Thomas," in Roman T. Ciapalo, ed., *Postmodernism and Christian Philosophy.* American Maritain Association. Washington D.C.: The Catholic University of America Press, 1997: 218–29.

Seeskin, Kenneth. "Maimonides on Creation," in Jospe, Raphael and Dov Schwartz, eds., *Jewish Philosophy: Perspectives and Retrospectives*. Brighton: Academic Studies Press, 2012: 185–99.

Sermoneta, Giuseppe. *Un glossario filosofico ebraico italiano del XIII secolo* [A Hebrew-Italian Philosophical Glossary of the 13th century]. Firenze: Olschki Editori, 1969.

Shelley, Mary Wollstonecraft. *Frankenstein or the Modern Prometheus* (Edited with an Introduction and Notes by M. K. Joseph). Oxford: Oxford University Press, 2008.

Shiffman, Mark. "What is Ideology?" *The Political Science Reviewer*, 46.2 (2022): 1–23.

Soars, Daniel. "Creation in Aquinas: Ex nihilo or ex deo?" *New Blackfriars*, 102.1102 (2020). https://doi.org/10.1111/nbfr.12603.

Sommavilla, Guido. *Il pensiero non è un labirinto: dialettica e mistero*. Milano: Jaca Book, 1981.

Strauss, Leo. *An Introduction to Political Philosophy: Ten Essays by Leo Strauss* (Edited with an Introduction by Hilail Gildin). Detroit: Wayne State University Press, 1989 [1975].

———. *Natural Right and History*. Chicago and London: Chicago University Press, 1965 [1950].

———. *Philosophy and Law: Contributions to the Understanding of Maimonides and His Predecessors* (*Philosophie und Gesetz*, 1935, Translated by Eve Adler). Albany: SUNY Press, 1995.

———. *Persecution and the Art of Writing*. Chicago and London: University of Chicago Press, 1988 [1952]

———. "Political Philosophy and History," *Journal of the History of Ideas*, 10.1 (1949): 30–50.

———. *The City and Man*. Chicago: University of Chicago Press, 1964.

———. "The Place of the Doctrine of Providence According to Maimonides" (Translated by Gabriel Bartlett and Svetozar Minkov; originally published in 1937 under the title, "Der Ort der Vorsehungslehre nach der Ansicht Maimunis)," *The Review of Metaphysics*, 57.3 (2004): 537–49.

Tabaczek, Mariusz OP. "Thomistic Response to the Theory of Evolution: Aquinas on Natural Selection and the Perfection of the Universe," *Theology and Science*, 13.3 (2015): 325–44.

Tamarchio, John, "The Emergence of the 'Supposit' in a Metaphysics of Creation," *Paper Presented at the Twentieth World Congress of Philosophy*. Boston, August 10–15, 1998 (Published in The Paideia Archives), at www.bu.edu/wcp/Papers/Medi/MediToma.htm.

Taylor, Richard C. "Primary Causality and Ibda'(creare) in the Liber de Causis," in *Wahrheit und Geschichte: Die gebrochene Tradition metaphysischen Denkens* (Festschrift zum 70: Geburtstag von Günther Mensching). Würzburg: Königshausen & Neumann, 2012: 115–36, at https://core.ac.uk/download/pdf/213075095.pdf.

Tkacz, Michael W. *Thomas Aquinas vs. The Intelligent Designers What is God's Finger Doing in My Pre-Biotic Soup?* March 15, 2007, at http://guweb2.gonzaga.edu/faculty/calhoun/socratic/Tkacz_AquinasvsID.html.

Torrell, Jean-Pierre. *Nouvelles Recherches Thomasiennes* (Bibliotheque Thomiste 61). Paris: Librerie Philosophique, J. Vrin, 2008.

———. *Saint Thomas d'Aquin, maître spirituel*. Paris: Cerf, Editions universitaires de Fribourg, 1996.
Vespignani, Alfonso Maria, Mons. *Dell'esemplarismo divino secondo i principi scientifici del Dottore S. Tommaso Aquinate*. Fiaccadori: Parma 1887.
Vico, Giambattista. "De Antiquissima Italorum Sapientia ex Linguae Latinae Originibus Eruenda," in Emanuela Sanna ed., *Of the Most-ancient Wisdom of Italians Unearthed from the Origins of the Latin Language*. Roma: Edizioni di Storia e Letteratura, 2005 [1710].
———. "De Nostri Temporis Studiorum Ratione," in *On Our Times' Way of Studying*. Roma: Edizioni di Storia e Letteratura, 2022 [1708].
———. *Principi di Scienza Nuova delle Nazioni* (1744), "Introduction," in Paolo Cristofolini and Manuela Sanna, eds., *La Scienza Nuova 1744*. Roma: Edizioni di Storia e Letteratura, 2013 (2015 ISPF edition at www.ispf-lab.cnr.it/2015_101.pdf).
Ward, John O. "What the Middle Ages Missed of Cicero, and Why," in William H.F. Altman, ed., *Brill's Companion to the Reception of Cicero* (Brill's Companions to Classical Reception Series. Vol. 2). Leiden and Boston: Brill, 2015.
Watts, Edward J. *The Eternal Decline and Fall of Rome: The History of a Dangerous Idea*. Oxford: Oxford University Press, 2021.
Whitehead, Alfred North. *Adventures of Ideas*. New York and London: The Free Press, 1967 [1933].
Wright, Edwin. "Creation and the Method of Saint Thomas Aquinas," at https://planegeodesy.com/appendix-i-creation-and-the-method-of-saint-thomas-aquinas; and "Evolutionism Refuted by the Ribosome," at https://planegeodesy.com/appendix-ii-evolutionism-refuted-by-the-ribosome.

# Index

Adam 3, 20, 54, 75, 86
Adam (Second) 20
Albertus Magnus, St. 29
Alston, William P. 12
Anaxagoras 13
anthropology 39, 75
Aquinas, Thomas St. 7, 10, 12–13, 18, 20, 28–32, 34–42, 45–6, 49–56, 58, 60, 64, 67–9, 71–2, 75, 78–84, 86, 88–93, 95–8
Aristophanes 22, 32
Aristotle (Stagirite, Peripatetic) ii, vii, xi, xiv, 2–3, 12–14, 19–21, 30–2, 34–6, 39, 48–50, 56, 65, 69, 74, 80, 82, 86–7, 89, 91, 97
Arnold, Matthew 15, 26
atheism ix, 25, 29, 55
Athens and Jerusalem 10, 19, 45, 84
Auerbach, Eric 20
Augustine, St. (Bishop of Hippo) v, 3–4, 9–10, 13, 19, 20, 27–9, 43, 45, 66, 76, 83, 95, 96
Averroës (Ibn Rushd) 36, 39, 46
Avicenna (Ibn Sina) 36–7, 68

Barrow, John D. and Tipler, Frank J. 14
Benjamin, Walter x
Bible *see* Torah/Bible
biology 11, 86–7
Blondel, Maurice 11
body (*sōma*) 3, 17, 22, 26, 41, 51, 74–5, 83–4, 90
Boethius 28, 45, 47–9, 56, 62–3, 65–9, 73–7, 89–90, 95, 97
Bonaventure St. 34, 44, 78, 81
Book of Causes (Liber de Causis, LDC) 67–8, 70, 92
Bradley, Denis J. M. 20
Butterworth, Charles E. 46

Caesar, Julius 37
chaos 17, 63, 65, 75, 93
Christian Platonism 3, 38
Christ 4, 18–20, 29, 53–4, 60, 65
Cicero 11–12, 15, 62, 63
Clarke, Norris 13
Constantine (Roman Emperor) 9

Damocles 8
Dante (Comedy, etc.) 4, 6, 9, 17–18, 20, 22, 28, 30, 45–6, 65, 77–8
Darwin 83, 90
Dawkins, Richard 23–5, 27
death of God 8–9, 38, 77–8, 82, 87
De Chardin, Teilhard 82
De Clairvaux Bernard 81
Deism 52, 78
Demiurge 84, 97
Democritus 18
Descartes (Cartesian) 2, 8, 12–13, 25, 31, 75
DeSpain, Benjamin R. 39
Doolan, Gregory T. xiv, 13, 32, 34–5, 38–9, 50
Dostoyevsky, Fyodor x
Duhem, Pierre 12, 34, 37, 38–40

*eîdos* (form) 2, 4, 10, 13–14, 26, 35–9, 49–50, 67, 69–70, 72, 76, 82–6, 88–94
emanation(ism) 41, 48–9, 51–4, 56, 60, 62, 64, 67–9, 73, 79–80, 86–8
emanation(ism) 48, 49, 51–4, 56, 60, 62–4, 67–9, 71, 73, 79–80, 86–8
Epicureanism 5
eternity 1–3, 6, 36, 44, 55, 69–71, 73–4, 79
ethics 27, 42, 45, 55, 87
eucharist 17, 44

Eve 75
evil x, xiii, 16, 18, 56–61, 74–6, 85, 93, 95–6
evolution(ism) ix–x, 25, 57, 73–4, 82–5, 86, 91
existentialism ix

Fabro, Cornelio 31
faith (*fides*) 11, 18–20, 39, 49, 69–70, 77, 80
freedom ix–x, 5, 11–12, 15–16, 20–1, 53–4, 56, 58–60, 65, 68, 70–80, 87–8

Galilei, Galileo 14–15, 87
Genesis (Bereshit) 55, 59, 93
Gerson, Lloyd P. 30
Gildin, Hilail 27
Gilson, Etienne 32
globalism 29, 82, 97
Gluck, Andrew xiv, 19, 27, 55
Gnosticism 4, 25
Gorgias (Sophist) 11, 18
Gospels (Acts) 5, 19–22, 30, 44, 48, 59, 65, 72, 75–6
Gravina Gian Vincenzo 15, 19
Greeks 17, 41–2, 89
Green, Kenneth Hart 45, 55, 70
Grotius 15

Hades 6
Hamlet 6
Hegel, Georg Wilhelm 12, 16, 20, 32
Heidegger, Martin 30
Henle, Robert John 30, 34, 38
Hibbs, Thomas S. 20
historicism 10–12, 20, 27, 32
history 8, 10–12, 14, 16, 19, 21, 27, 32, 34–6, 41, 77
Hobbes, Thomas 6, 15, 24
*homo faber* 12
Husserl, Edmund 14, 26

ideals 41, 52, 77–8, 97
ideas (eternal) ix, 1–3, 8–10, 13, 33–5, 38–9, 41, 47, 48, 50, 67, 70, 88, 89–90, 93, 97–8
ideology ix–x, 4–5, 7–8, 10, 14, 25–6, 29, 34, 39
imitation 16, 18, 39–40, 47, 67, 76, 78, 84
Intelligent Design 12, 82, 84, 86

Jesus *see* Christ
Jews (Hebrews) 59

Jolivet, Régis 29, 60, 84
Joseph (Jesus's Father) 53

Kant, Immanuel ix, 5–6, 20, 26, 38–9, 50, 77, 87
Klein, Jacob 19, 31
Krauss, Lawrence 23–5
Kretzmann, Norman 7, 12–13

Langiulli, Nino 7
law (*nomos*) 2–4, 6, 9–12, 15, 19, 26, 39, 42, 46, 62
Lewis, C.S. 16
*libido dominandi* 28
Limbo 77
Logos 5, 18–19, 25, 48, 56, 62, 67, 74–8, 80
Lombard, Peter 28, 45, 49, 56–9, 61, 68, 83–5
Lucifer 17, 61, 76
Lundy, Steven 9

Machiavelli, Niccolò 3, 5–6, 8, 14–16, 26, 85, 87
MacIntyre, Alasdair 14
Maimonides, xiv, 10, 19, 27, 39–40, 45, 50, 55, 57, 70
materialism 2, 26, 71, 86, 89
matter 14, 36, 49, 51–2, 58, 63, 69, 75–6, 83–5
metaphysics 26, 63, 84, 91
Michelangelo (Buonarroti) 17
mind xiii, 2, 4–5, 8, 10, 12–14, 16–17, 19–20, 22, 27, 34–5, 38, 44–5, 47, 50, 60, 62–3, 66, 67, 69, 73–6, 78, 80, 93, 97–8
miracles ix
misanthropy 14, 18, 24–5
Molière 22

Nagel, Thomas x, 11–12
naturalism 12
nature (*physis*) 2–12, 16, 18–20, 24, 28, 30, 31, 34, 40–1, 42, 47, 48, 51, 52, 54, 56, 59, 67, 82–8, 90–1, 93
Neo-Platonism 37, 68
Nietzsche, Friedrich 6, 30, 78, 85

Oakeshott, Michael 27
Ovid 18
Owens, Joseph 35

# 108  Index

participation (in divine providence or intellective agency) xiv, 20, 29, 31, 39, 45, 47, 56, 67–8, 79–80, 87, 92
patristic 30, 45
Paul, St. (Ephesians, etc.) 3, 19, 21–2, 28, 48, 59, 65, 75
Petrarch, Francesco 4, 16
philology ix, 7–11, 13, 28–9
Pico della Mirandola 54
Plato/Platonism/Platonic 1–4, 7, 10–13, 15, 17–20, 22, 27–32, 35–42, 44–5, 49–50, 53–4, 60, 67–8, 70, 71, 74, 78–80, 82, 85–6, 89–90, 92–5, 97–8
Plato (Timaeus etc.) 2
Plotinus 67–8
poetic reason 3, 8–9, 11, 15–16, 20, 22, 25, 30–1, 37, 42, 55, 78
poetry 4, 9, 15, 17–19, 37, 47, 56, 87
positivism 38, 40
Proclus/Proclean 67–8
Protagoras 7
Protestant(ism) 82, 84
providence (divine and human) 9–11, 13, 21, 28–9, 34–5, 42, 46, 48, 52, 54–7, 59, 62, 70, 73, 75–7, 80–1, 83, 88, 90–1
Puritans 84

Rahner Karl 11, 21
Renaissance 15, 22
Resurrection 5–6, 74
Roman empire 4, 8–9, 14
Romantic(ism) 16–17, 85
Romulus 3
Rovighi, Sofia Vanni 39

Saint-Exupéry, Antoine de 23
Schall James V. SJ xiv
science (modern) 2, 6, 8–9, 15, 23, 25–6, 47, 60, 77, 82–3, 92

Scipio 63
Seeskin, Kenneth 55
Shakespeare, William 3, 5–6, 9, 16
Soars 62–3, 69, 73
Socrates 3, 12–13, 18, 22, 32, 35, 38, 41, 45
soul 18, 37, 41, 57, 70, 83, 89
Spinoza 1, 8, 15, 20, 87
Stoicism 5, 22
Strauss, Leo 8, 10, 14, 30, 39–40, 45, 70, 84

Tabaczek, Mariusz OP 91
Taylor, Richard C. 68
technology/technocracy x, 9, 14, 60, 85, 87, 97
Thrasymachus 11
Tkacz, Michael W. 90
Torah/Bible 6, 12, 27, 30, 42, 45, 55–6, 70, 90, 93, 97
Torrell Jean-Pierre 27, 32, 38, 41–2, 44, 54
trans-modernism x
Trinity 39, 52, 56, 84

Varro 3, 9
Vico, Giambattista 8–9, 11, 13–16, 19–20, 29, 40
Voltaire 19
voluntarism 70, 80, 82, 84

*Weltanschauung* 14
Whitehead Alfred N. 1
world/order (*mundus*) 1–5, 7, 15–18, 23–4, 27, 33, 37, 48–50, 52, 54–5, 59–60, 62–3, 65, 69, 71, 73, 75–6, 78, 85–9, 91, 97

Zeus 97–8

For Product Safety Concerns and Information please contact our EU representative  GPSR@taylorandfrancis.com
Taylor & Francis Verlag GmbH, Kaufingerstraße 24, 80331 München, Germany

www.ingramcontent.com/pod-product-compliance
Lightning Source LLC
Chambersburg PA
CBHW051754230426
43670CB00012B/2287